R. T. Kendall is an inspiration to young and old. His biblical teaching combines theological intellect with deep wisdom and the power of the Holy Spirit. No wonder so many love to read his books and hear him preach.

– Nicky Gumbel

Wisdom is priceless. Knowing how to get it shou
exper ive. But it isn't, because R.T. shows us the
warr ngaging and vital book. Be very wise. Bu

A sh   and stimulating study of a neglectec
welco   book of wisdom on wisdom!

– Revd Canon J. John

Utter   mpelling.

– Rob Parsons

I am s   rateful for this book. It has provoked in me a fresh desire to know   e wisdom of God. We have available to us today great stores of kno edge, but without wisdom, we gain little. Our longing for it drives   back to God. Read this and find a treasure map!

– Canon Nick Cuthbert

'Brill   ' 'superb,' 'excellent.' Often, such preaching commendations conv   ore about style than content. 'Wise,' on the other hand, deals more   h the divine touch than the human craft. R. T. Kendall is a very wise   – and not just in his preaching. A book like this has double value,   wisdom is a rare gift that is best taught by the wise. I would not want   to miss this book. That could be very foolish indeed.

– Dr Clive Calver

Our   esent age has a voracious appetite for the power of information and enjoys unprecedented access to it, but the wisdom to know how to   e it is not nearly as abundant. Those who hunger for wisdom that i not only ageless and trustworthy but also practical will find this   ok an invaluable resource in their quest.

– Graham Kendrick

Masterful. Nobody should be without this book.

– Colin Dye

Also by R. T. Kendall

The Anointing
The Christian and the Pharisee (with David Rosen)
Did You Think To Pray?
The Excellent Way
The Gift of Giving
The Lord's Prayer
Out of the Comfort Zone
Pure Joy
Second Chance
The Sin No One Talks About (Jealousy)
Thanking God
Total Forgiveness
Totally Forgiving Ourselves
The Scandal of Christianity
Totally Forgiving God

In Pursuit
of His Wisdom

R. T. KENDALL

HODDER &
STOUGHTON

Unless indicated otherwise, Scripture quotations are taken from the
Holy Bible, New International Version (Anglicised edition).
Copyright © 1979, 1984, 2011 by Biblica (formerly International
Bible Society). Used by permission. All rights reserved.

First published in Great Britain in 2014 by Hodder & Stoughton
An Hachette UK company

1

A CIP catalogue record for this title is available from the British Library

ISBN 978 1 444 74972 4
eBook ISBN 978 1 444 74973 1

Typeset in Sabon by Hewer Text UK Ltd, Edinburgh

Printed and bound in the UK by Clays Ltd, St Ives plc

Hodder & Stoughton policy is to use papers that are natural, renewable
and recyclable products and made from wood grown in sustainable
forests. The logging and manufacturing processes are expected to
conform to the environmental regulations of the country of origin.

Hodder & Stoughton Ltd
338 Euston Road
London NW1 3BH

www.hodderfaith.com

To

Judith and Victor

Contents

Preface

Many years ago when on holiday in Florida my wife Louise punctured her ear drum. The first Sunday back at Westminster Chapel she happened to sit next to a young lady – Judith – who was deaf. For some reason Louise knew instantly that she should learn sign language. She did, and the eventual result was that Louise started a signing ministry to deaf people. During this same era a young man named Victor also felt inspired to learn signing. He did, and became a brilliant signer. The truth was, though, he had his eye on Judith! His plan worked, and it was my pleasure to take the wedding of Judith and Victor a few years later.

While at Westminster Chapel I preached through 1 Corinthians. When we came to 1 Corinthians 12:8–10 (the section on the gifts of the Holy Spirit) I spent the entire sermon on the first gift listed – wisdom. After the service Judith came to me and said, 'Would you please consider writing a book on wisdom?' She may have forgotten this, but I didn't. It has been on my list as a book I wanted to write for many years – and Judith will no doubt be surprised to learn that I have dedicated this book to both her and Victor.

In the year 2000, Hodder & Stoughton asked me to write a book describing my ministry at Westminster Chapel. It came out in early 2002, coinciding with our departure from the Chapel. I called the book *In Pursuit of His Glory* – and it was an honest description of my efforts during those twenty-five years. While writing the present book, it came to me that I should call it *In Pursuit of His Wisdom*. Like the glory of God, we can only pursue it. We will not come to the end of that pursuit until we see Christ face to face and are like him (1 John 3:3). So too with wisdom. Christ's wisdom is imputed to us when we trust his death on the cross (1 Cor. 1:30) – and imparted to us only in measure in the here and now. But one day we shall know God's wisdom in a manner impossible to grasp on this earth. We only pursue it. That is what this book is about.

I am so grateful for friends like Rob Parsons and Lyndon and Celia Bowring for reading the manuscript. I thank Lyndon for writing the Foreword and Celia for her help, particularly regarding the sections that deal with women in Scripture.

I want to thank Ian Metcalf at Hodder for publishing this book, and I particularly want to thank my brilliant editor Katherine Venn for her wisdom in this my latest literary venture. She has been my editor before, and I am thrilled to have her counsel once again. My deepest thanks, as always, are to Louise – my best friend and critic.

It is my prayer that this book will bless you and help you in your own search for true wisdom.

R. T. Kendall
January 2014
Nashville, Tennessee

Foreword

This book is vintage R.T. It is dripping with scripture – as you would expect from someone who immerses himself in The Word and then seeks to expound theological truth in ways that will build you up and transform your life. As a close friend I am privileged to observe R.T. at very close quarters as we enjoy spending days of retreat together; this beautiful book reflects his deep longing to know God more, to see His wisdom outworked in his life and yours. R.T.'s strong desire to know God's wisdom has taken him on a journey through the Bible to discover how we can understand more of God's will and God's ways. Readers of R.T.'s books will know of his honesty regarding his personal limitations and his determination by the grace of God to overcome his weaknesses.

In Pursuit of His Wisdom addresses our daily need to know the Holy Spirit's mind, thus identifying His will and receiving His guidance so we can think, speak and act in ways that please and glorify God. True wisdom begins with a wholesome and healthy fear of the Lord. He helps us to bring the wisdom of God into our praying: exercising faith, accepting how He answers, and understanding that sometimes we need to wait patiently for His perfect timing. As you apply these truths I believe you will experience a fresh hunger to encounter God more intimately and understand more of His wisdom. R.T. also unpacks the importance of avoiding unguarded comments that can cause such damage, and identifies some of the great heroes of the Bible – giants in the realm of knowing God but equally capable of making mistakes.

The wisdom of the Spirit is at odds with how this world operates, and of course we are constantly affected by the thinking and motivation of self; but God's wisdom can change us – as Romans 12 says, we can be counter cultural, transformed by the 'renewing of our minds'. In our hurting world where pride, selfishness and injustice abounds we are desperately in need of Christians who will seek after God's wisdom and live it out in the workplace, the public square, family life and every other aspect of contemporary culture.

The greatest expression of God's wisdom is the gospel of salvation. Paul observed that the cross of Christ is regarded by many as utter foolishness, yet its glorious truth is central to all biblical truth and the more we fathom the depths of the truth of Jesus' death, resurrection and ascension the wiser we will become.

Is there anything in the universe that is purer and more wonderful than the wisdom of God?

I believe reading and inwardly digesting this book will result in your experiencing a deepening walk with God: not just learning more about Him, but truly knowing Him more intimately – He who is all wisdom.

– Lyndon Bowring

Introduction

How much better to get wisdom than gold, to
get insight rather than silver! (Prov. 16:16)

The beginning of wisdom is this: Get wisdom, and
whatever you get, get insight. (Prov. 4:7, ESV)

It is an audacious step to write a book on wisdom. Does
writing a book on this subject imply that the author has
wisdom? No – only a fool would be so pretentious as to
think so. Paul cautioned: 'Never be wise in your own sight'
(Rom. 12:16, ESV), a verse we must never forget.

And yet a book on wisdom is needed if it can help someone to become wiser.

I am now old, but being old is no guarantee of wisdom.
A lesson to be learned from Shakespeare's *King Lear* is that
there is no fool like an old fool. I've known a lot of people
who seemed to get sillier rather than wiser as they grew
older. I recently had a person come to me and say, 'It is so
good to meet someone who is finishing well.' I tried to
smile. I certainly want to end well, but I am not finished

1

yet. I have not arrived. I am learning every day. Paul feared he could still be disqualified for the prize at the judgment seat of Christ: 'I strike a blow to my body and make it my slave so that after I have preached to others, I myself will not be disqualified for the prize' (1 Cor. 9:27). That was written in about AD 55. But some ten years later he was prepared to say, 'I have finished the race, I have kept the faith. Now there is in store for me the crown of righteousness' (2 Tim. 4:7–8). He was confident in the end. Perhaps a few years from now I might venture to write a book on finishing well – but not today.

So please do not take the title of this book to suggest to you that I am an expert on this subject. I am in pursuit of wisdom. I am the expert on making foolish mistakes – and I have even learned from some of them. I only pray that my years of experience will contribute in measure to the writing of this book.

My family and I moved to England in 1973, not for me to become the minister of Westminster Chapel but to do research at Oxford. For the next three years I was privileged to be mentored by some of the greatest minds in the world – these being not only my supervisor Dr Barrie White, but also Dr J. I. Packer and Dr Martyn Lloyd-Jones. These three men monitored the writing of my D.Phil. thesis, but one day I was shaken rigid by the most humbling and embarrassing advice I have ever been given. During the course of lunch Dr Packer said to Dr White, 'Shall you tell him or shall I?' Jim Packer then turned to me to say as gently as he could that I was not going to do the thesis I had come to England specifically for. I had told all my friends I was doing a thesis on the Puritan John Owen. But Dr Packer and Dr White had to break the news to me that I should 'limit my liabilities' – a polite way of saying I was a long way from doing the D.Phil. unless I radically changed direction. I died a thousand deaths when I heard this, and went to bed with a migraine – fearing my world had collapsed.

It was in fact the best thing that happened to me at Oxford. *Wisdom prevailed*. They demonstrated wisdom in breaking the news, and I finally had the wisdom to agree with them. The result was that I was saved from being a hard, cold, reformed theologian and was made into a softer, gentler preacher of the gospel.

It is one thing to have wisdom when needing to know the next step forward, but another to recognise another's wisdom when they are trying to show you something. But it can also be devastating to your pride.

We will see more than one definition of wisdom in this book. But in the present context I would define wisdom simply as saying or doing the right thing – and at the right time. Not saying or doing the right thing shows our lack of wisdom. Even the correct thing said at the *wrong* time may show lack of wisdom.

Ultimate wisdom

The unveiling of the greatest secret and greatest wisdom – God's infinite purpose and plan – is the reason he sent his Son into the world to die on a cross. Jesus Christ shed his blood for our redemption. If we miss that we have missed everything. But if we *do* grasp that, we are in a position to move on towards other levels of God's wisdom. Dr Martyn Lloyd-Jones always stressed the importance of going 'from the general to the particular'. We are not wise to jump to particulars – 'What job should I have? Should I get married? What is my calling? What should I do next?' – unless we have accepted the greatest wisdom of all – namely, the knowledge of God's plan of redemption. As we will see below, God kept this secret wisdom from Satan; but it is now revealed to all who will accept it.

Jesus always said and did the right thing. However, he never spoke or did anything on his own: 'The Son can do nothing by himself; he can do only what he sees his Father doing, because whatever the Father does the Son also does' (John 5:19). Jesus' words and deeds mirrored the Father's perfect wisdom, and he never spoke what was untrue, unguarded or unwise. He never uttered a comment then later said, 'Oh dear, I wish I hadn't said that'; or had to say, 'Sorry, I do apologize'. James said, 'Anyone who is never at fault in what they say is perfect, able to keep their whole body in check' (Jas. 3:2). But Jesus the God-man *was* perfect, never sinning – ever – in thought, word and deed. Tempted? Yes. But he was without sin (Heb. 4:15).

You and I are not perfect – nor will we ever be in this present life. But at the same time we are called to seek after wisdom. Wisdom is 'supreme' – the greatest good we can seek, the most noble virtue there is, the greatest gift that is on offer, and the highest plateau for living available in this present world. That said, what James calls wisdom is much the same as what Paul calls *agape* love in 1 Corinthians 13. They are not always the same, but they can come close. *Agape* love is distinguished from the Greek word *philia* – brotherly love – and *eros* – physical love. Agape love is selfless concern – unselfish caring. It is kind, not self-seeking, and keeps no record of wrongs (1 Cor. 13:4–5). So too is the wisdom that comes from heaven – pure, peace-loving and full of mercy (Jas. 3:17). Furthermore, what John calls 'perfect love' comes close to the same thing as the wisdom depicted by James.

Wisdom focuses on knowing the next step forward in making decisions, knowing what is the mind of the Holy Spirit, and avoiding the unguarded comment. That is what this book is about.

The purpose of this book

The purpose of this book therefore is an attempt to motivate you both to want and seek what Proverbs calls 'supreme' and to see the value of this wisdom. A subsidiary benefit, should it emerge, would be seeing a way forward on how to acquire wisdom. In the meantime, listen to Solomon who allegedly wrote much of Proverbs: 'Cherish her, and she will exalt you; embrace her, and she will honour you. She will give you a garland to grace your head and present you with a glorious crown' (Prov. 4:8–9). Therefore you and I are admonished to 'get' wisdom: 'Though it cost all you have, get understanding' (Prov. 4:7). But as we will see below, it does 'cost'.

It is a sign of wisdom itself if one chooses it over and above anything else in life. It is a sign of folly to choose anything *other* than wisdom – whether it be riches, people's approval, success, prestige, carnal pleasure, great achievements, fame, friends or even good health.

Definitions of wisdom

Wisdom is getting God's opinion, for true wisdom *is* God's opinion. God's glory is his opinion. The root word of the Greek *doxa* – 'glory' – means 'opinion', so true wisdom, then, is God's opinion. God *always* has an opinion on any matter. He therefore should be consulted first when we want to know the next step forward.

God's wisdom exists on two levels: general and particular. His general wisdom is his Word – Holy Scripture – and the more we know and embrace his Word, the greater the likelihood is that we will demonstrate wisdom. Particular wisdom is knowing the next step forward in our lives.

Dr Michael Eaton reckons that wisdom is possessing 'the ability to get things done'. There are those people in life who can be entrusted with responsibility to carry out an order so that you never need to ask whether something has been done. Some people can make things happen; some can't. My father used to say to me, 'If you want something done, ask a busy person to do it.'

Wisdom is knowing the next step forward in what we say or do. *Timing* is an essential ingredient in the unfolding of wisdom. There can be a wrong time to say what may otherwise be 100 per cent correct. Knowing when to speak is part of the glory of wisdom. Wisdom can also be defined as having 20/20 foresight vision. Many of us have 20/20 hindsight vision; we can see – often too late – what we *should* have done. But wisdom is making the right decision in advance. It is like seeing the end from the beginning – which of course only God can do. But when true wisdom sets in, it is as though you know in advance exactly what to say or do. To put it another way, wisdom is having the ability to do what you will be glad you did.

My own definition of wisdom is having *the presence of the mind of the Holy Spirit*. His timing is always perfect, because the Holy Spirit always knows what to do next. You may have messed up yesterday – or an hour ago – but what should you do *now*? Answer: only the Holy Spirit knows. I compare it to my Sat Nav in my car. The voice clearly says, 'In one hundred yards turn right'. But you drive on – and miss the turning. What does the voice say then – 'I told you to turn right, you stupid twit'? No, the calm voice merely says 'Recalculating'. There is no moralising, no being told off. The Holy Spirit does not shout 'I told you so' when we err. His voice calmly tells you what to do *now*. So if you have the mind of the Spirit, you know what to do right now. You may have made a mistake, but the Holy Spirit *always* knows what to do now. God does not 'preach' to us when we have blown it. He knows our frame and remembers that we are dust (Ps. 103:14). Jesus is touched with the feeling of our weaknesses (Heb. 4:15, AV). Instead of making us feel guilty and rubbing our noses in it, he gently tells us what to do *next*.

What is most thrilling to me is that wisdom is not only on offer, but that God *delights* in giving us wisdom – that is, showing the next step forward in what to do. We may need to know the next step forward generally or particularly. For example, the next step forward generally would refer to major decisions for the future – God's will for our lives; our calling in life; the right place to live; the right job; whether to marry. God only wants what is best for us; he will show us his plan in more detail if we truly want to know what it is. Paul said we should not be unwise, but instead know what God's will is (Eph. 5:17).

The next step forward could refer to the next minute or so. When we have erred in a particular moment, we may say, 'Oh dear, I have just blown it. What can I do now?' The good news is that God can help us to know what to say or do *immediately*. I myself know what it is for him to come down mercifully and bail me out! It *may* involve having to apologise – or ask for forgiveness. And if we truly want wisdom in a given moment, it may mean having to lose face. But having the presence of the mind of the Holy Spirit is pure gold and far outweighs the embarrassment of having messed up or having to apologise. It is not that God necessarily *tells* us to apologise in a way that is embarrassing; instead he has a way of making us see for ourselves that – sometimes – the best thing to do is to admit when we have got it wrong. But in his infinite wisdom he has a way of showing us the next step forward, without forcing us. God doesn't compel us against our will, but makes us willing to go.

Etymology and wisdom

The word 'wisdom' comes from the Hebrew *chokmah* (which means 'prudence', 'leading the heart in the right way') and the Greek *sophia* (as in the Septuagint, the Greek translation of the Hebrew Old Testament, and the New Testament). In the ancient Hellenistic world *sophia* was considered to be a gift of divine grace, the possession of the gods alone. In other words, it was seen to be out of reach for ordinary human beings. But in the Bible wisdom is something we should not only desire, but expect; and it is to our peril not to seek it. James 3:15–18 makes a distinction between the wisdom that is from below (demonic, leading to selfish ambition and 'every evil practice') and that which is from above (heavenly, leading to 'righteousness'). There are various shades and uses of *chokmah* and *sophia*. But the heavenly 'wisdom from above' is what is meant in this book by 'wisdom', whether in Proverbs, James or anywhere else in the Bible.

The word 'understanding' is also relevant. 'Wisdom' and 'understanding' are often used interchangeably (Prov. 4:7; Prov. 16:16), but the Hebrew word *biynah* – 'understanding' – may also mean 'discernment'. It translates into the Greek *suniemi* – 'to understand' – but it also means 'to come together'. When things 'come together' you are able to understand, and it ultimately means to understand God's will. As I just mentioned, Paul cautions us not to be unwise, but to understand what the will of the Lord is (Eph. 5:17). Jesus opened the disciples' minds that they might 'understand' the Scriptures. So when we are urged to get wisdom, to get 'understanding', we are aiming for the highest privilege on offer from God to his people. Wisdom is supreme, more precious than gold; understanding is more precious than silver (Prov. 16:16).

Many verses in Proverbs warn us against rejecting God's wisdom. If we persistently reject his knowledge, we will sooner or later experience indescribable sorrow and regret. The consequence could be that we become stone deaf to God's voice – or that God himself will actually stop speaking to us. This could mean having a mind incapable of clear thinking – a reprobate mind (Rom. 1:28). The worst thing that can happen to you or me therefore is to be forever unable to grasp God's will, to be completely unable to understand God's Word, and utterly incapable of knowing the next step forward in our lives. People like this are described in Hebrews 6:4–6; they were never to be granted repentance again. It was actually *impossible* for them to repent again. Therefore we are urged to seek this wisdom and understanding as long as we can hear God's voice.

The consequences for not doing this are horrible: for God will 'laugh' at our disaster and 'mock' when calamity overtakes us – all because we did not choose the fear of the Lord (Prov. 1:26–27, 29). I cannot think of anything scarier than this, and this is why not making wisdom our utmost priority is to invite trouble of incalculable proportions. I urge you therefore to take seriously what the Bible says about wisdom – what it will do for us when we make it our utmost priority, and what happens when we reject God's warnings concerning it.

The wonderful thing is, God offers us wisdom – and delights in giving it. I pray that you will be impelled to seek God's opinion on everything that touches your life. Having to accept God's wisdom can be humbling; it can hurt our pride. But we have to remember that God only wants what is best for us – and we need to grasp his offer of wisdom with both hands.

1

A Wise Choice

The fear of the LORD is the beginning
of wisdom, and knowledge of the Holy
One is understanding. (Prov. 9:10)

. . . since you disregard all my advice and do
not accept my rebuke, I in turn will laugh
when disaster strikes you; I will mock when
calamity overtakes you . . . [Because you] did not
choose to fear the LORD . . . (Prov. 1:25–26, 29)

I have some good news – wisdom is not far away. It is not
for the 'gods' alone, as the ancient Greeks reckoned. It is
not for the 'Platos' and 'Aristotles' of this world. It is on
offer to all of us – to ordinary people like you and me. In
fact, it is closer than our hands or our feet, closer than the
air we breathe. For wisdom is the result of a choice we can
make – it starts with an act of the will. It is like total forgiveness; we choose whether or not to forgive totally.

In the Introduction I suggested several definitions of
wisdom:

- It is seeing why God sent his Son into the world.
- It is having God's opinion on any matter.
- It is discerning the presence of the mind of the Holy Spirit.
- It is knowing the next step forward regarding what we do.
- It is saying the right thing at the right time.
- It is having the ability to get things done.
- It is choosing wisdom above anything else in life.

The fear of the Lord: choosing God's opinion

How do you get wisdom? *By choosing the fear of the Lord.* As we shall see in more detail below, this means that you so respect God's ways as revealed in his Word that you value and seek his opinion on any issue, above any other perspective. Wisdom comes from making a calculated, strategic choice by an act of the will. It is not that you merely say, 'I choose wisdom' – as if to verbalise a wish. Note the order: you choose what Proverbs calls 'the fear of the Lord'. Wisdom follows. The fear of the Lord means choosing God's opinion over anyone else's – on any matter. The reason I emphasise this so soon and so strongly is because the book of Proverbs (known universally as *the* handbook of wisdom in the Bible) makes an inseparable connection between wisdom and the fear of the Lord. 'The fear of the LORD is the beginning of wisdom' (Prov. 9:10). Job agrees:

'The fear of the Lord – that is wisdom, and to shun evil is understanding' (Job 28:28). But it is a choice we must make.

It is the wisest choice you will ever make.

What is therefore so encouraging is that wisdom is clearly available to all of us – not merely the privileged or the elite. It begins not with good breeding, but with the fear of the Lord. The simplest and most ordinary person on the planet is invited to enter the arena of greatness – the obtaining of true wisdom. Few get there – but all are capable of it. Indeed, those who 'hated knowledge and did not *choose* to fear the LORD' are those who suffer the consequences of having God turn his back on them when trouble comes (Prov. 1:29 – my italics). The result of not having wisdom can be pretty awful, as we will see in more detail below.

Important clarification

However, choosing the fear of the Lord does not mean running scared day and night. It does not mean 'I choose to be afraid of God'. It is not living in perpetual terror that you have done something wrong and God is no longer speaking to you. It is not biting your nails regarding whether God is pleased or upset with you – like picking the petals off a daisy, saying, 'He loves me, he loves me not'. Away with the notion that God is always looking for a way to throw the book at us!

Wisdom means seeking his opinion, and choosing the fear of the Lord is precisely that. It is also seeking his timing as to when to speak or act. God has a point of view on everything, and he waits to be consulted before we make major decisions. It is our job to consult him. One of my favourite verses in the Bible is this: '. . . in all your ways submit to him, and he will make your paths straight' (Prov. 3:6). It cannot get more encouraging than that. This means to share your plans with God – to talk to him about anything and everything. Hide nothing from him. He is your friend, not your enemy. He loves being asked before we make major decisions. He likes being 'in' with us before anyone else is. Take him into your confidence. The fear of the Lord is consciously respecting that God can bless or withhold blessing as we show reverence for his perspective – that is, his Word and his ways.

One of the ancient prophets lamented that the people of God 'rejected knowledge' (Hos. 4:6). This does not mean they rejected education or did not go to university. That particular generation of ancient Israel rejected God's Word and ways, as we shall see further on in this chapter. I have been to countries where people can't get Bibles. I once gave a man a New Testament in a particular country, and he wept. He held on to it as if it were pure gold. Do you have a Bible? Do you read it? It is 'wisdom' to do that and 'wisdom' flows from that.

What if God had said that we get wisdom by having great brains? How would you feel if God had said:

- 'By education you get wisdom'?
- 'By being cultured you get wisdom'?
- 'By intellect, intelligence or a high IQ you get wisdom'?
- 'By success in making money you get wisdom'?
- 'By becoming knowledgeable in politics you get wisdom'?
- 'By seeking a political office and succeeding you get wisdom'?
- 'By being well connected you get wisdom'?
- 'By reading books on wisdom you get wisdom'?
- 'By hard work and experience you get wisdom'?
- 'By learning to play the piano or a musical instrument you get wisdom'?
- 'By reading *How to Win Friends and Influence People* you get wisdom'?

But no, acquiring wisdom is none of these. Thank God. It is the *fear of the Lord* that leads to wisdom, and it is *choosing* the fear of the Lord that results in wisdom. This leaves all of us without an excuse. We can't blame our brains, lack of learning, or not being born into a position of privilege. It is level ground; we *all* qualify.

The passive fear of the Lord

The fear of the Lord, however, may be understood in two ways: (1) a choice we make – wanting his opinion; and (2) a passive sense of the fear of the Lord – an unsought feeling.

It is of vital importance that we grasp (2) as well as (1); the passive fear of God demonstrates that we are talking about the *living* God. This means God can roll up his sleeves as if to say 'Enough is enough' – and answer prayer, or even bring judgment. When we realise that God is the same yesterday, today and for ever, we should be all the more motivated to choose the fear of the Lord.

Whereas the wisdom we are in pursuit of – the subject of this book – comes as the consequence of a *choice*, there have been occasions when the unsought passive fear of God was experienced. In the latter case, then, it is not the result of choice, but a *feeling*. It is sudden, unexpected. It is the experienced *awe* of God. In other words, it just happened!

How can this be? What is it like? Answer: it is when God steps in supernaturally. Here are three examples:

First, passive fear may emerge when God does something wonderful and extraordinary. That should bring great joy, and yet, strange as it may seem, it may bring fear. When Moses' face was radiant the people were 'afraid to come near him' (Exod. 34:30). When God answered Daniel's prayer, he 'stood up trembling' (Dan. 10:11). When Zechariah saw the angel of the Lord in the temple – who brought good news of answered prayer – he was 'gripped with fear' (Luke 1:12). When Jesus healed a paralytic, the people were 'filled with awe' (Luke 5:26). The women who saw and heard the angel at the empty tomb of Jesus on Easter Day were 'afraid yet filled with joy' (Matt. 28:8).

Second, passive fear may come upon people when God brings judgment – and shows his displeasure. The Mosaic Law was God's judgment upon Israel for their transgressions (Gal. 3:19). When the people heard the thunder, saw the lightning, heard the trumpet, and saw the mountain in smoke, 'they trembled with fear' (Exod. 20:18). When Uzzah touched the Ark of God – and was struck down dead – King David was 'afraid of the LORD that day' (2 Sam. 6:9). When Ananias and Sapphira were struck dead for lying to the Holy Spirit, 'great fear seized all who heard what had happened'; indeed such fear 'seized the whole church and all who heard about these events' (Acts 5:5, 11). One might surmise that such a scary and solemn scene would put people off – and drive them from coming to church. Yet the opposite happened (see Acts 5:12ff).

Third, the passive fear of God may come from anointed preaching. Like the two previously mentioned examples, this does not happen very often. But it is unforgettable when it does take place. It happened under the preaching of John the Baptist. We sometimes forget that one of the earliest messages of the New Testament – if not the first – was to 'flee from the coming wrath' (Matt. 3:7). Part of the fallout of John's preaching was that people came from as far away as Jerusalem (walking twenty miles) to hear him.

It is sometimes thought even today that preaching about 'the wrath of God' drives people away from churches. I would only observe that there is less preaching of this today than ever, and church attendance, speaking generally, is lower than ever. A sense of the fear of God was part of the fall-out from Peter's preaching on the Day of Pentecost (Acts 2:43). The high-water mark of the Great Awakening in New England in the USA came when Jonathan Edwards preached a memorable sermon ('Sinners in the hands of an angry God') on 8 July 1741 in Enfield, Connecticut. So great was the awe of God from this sermon that it was said that people were holding on to their pews to keep them from sliding into hell, and men outside were seen holding on to tree trunks for the same reason. This passive fear was experienced again in Bourbon County, Kentucky, in August 1801. A crowd of 15,000 in an area called Cane Ridge listened to a Methodist lay preacher as he took his text from 2 Corinthians 5:10: 'For we must all appear before the judgment seat of Christ, so that each of us may receive what is due to us for the things done while in the body, whether good or bad.' Hundreds passively fell to the ground, as did hundreds more over the following four days. But the long-term effect of the Cane Ridge Revival – called America's Second Great Awakening – lasted for years.

The primacy of the Word

As we have repeatedly said, the way forward in finding wisdom is to *choose* the fear of the Lord; that is, to seek his opinion on any matter.

But how, then, do you and I choose the fear of the Lord?

First, by choosing to be governed by the Word of God. There are two words in the Greek that can be translated 'word' – *logos* and *rhema*. The words are sometimes used interchangeably; therefore one must not press the distinction between them too far. But, generally speaking, *logos* refers to Holy Scripture; and *rhema* to a specific word of knowledge by the Spirit – a prophetic word. I fear there has been an unhealthy interest in the *rhema* word in some quarters these days, and some people are keen to get an immediate word – a word relevant to their situation – far more than the long-term reading and meditating on Scripture. It is like choosing McDonald's or Kentucky Fried Chicken instead of a gourmet restaurant. So many of us nowadays don't like having to wait very long! So a *rhema* word might tell me something I want to know in my situation *right now*.

Choosing the fear of the Lord should be a long-term commitment to get to know God by reading the Bible, and this takes time. But if we make the choice to know God's Word – Scripture – the reward down the line is incalculable. There is no substitute for the vast and deep knowledge of the Bible. This is the way you get to know the will of God generally. The more you know the Bible, the less you will feel the need for a 'quick word' in the moment.

I urge you to have a Bible reading plan. One-year Bible reading plans are easy to find and will keep you immersed in the Word. It takes approximately ten to twelve minutes a day (roughly four chapters a day) to stick to a one-year plan. You will never be sorry, and the result will be wisdom.

Yes, this is guaranteed. By committing yourself to know God's Word – and following it – will mean you will wear 'a garland to grace your head' (Prov. 4:9).

God's ways

Second, we show we have chosen the fear of the Lord by a commitment to know God's *ways*. God was grieved that his ancient people did not know his 'ways' (Heb. 3:10). You may not particularly like God's ways – at first. Some people resent the fact that God is a jealous God – his name is 'Jealous' (Exod. 34:14). But be glad about it, because it shows how much he loves you. His ways, though, are higher than our ways (Isa. 55:6), so we don't always understand what God is up to in our lives. But the more we know God's ways, the less surprised we are when disappointment comes or evil things happen in the world.

So how do you get to know God's ways? Answer: the same way that you get to know anybody's ways – by spending time with that person. Children often spell 'love' T–I–M–E. What if God spells our love for him like that? So may I ask you a specific question about your own personal quiet time? How much do you pray? In my book *Did You Think to Pray?* I focus a lot on how much time we spend with God. God likes your company, and he loves it when you like his as well. What is more, the devil doesn't like it when you spend *any time at all* with God.

Satan trembles when he sees
The weakest saint upon his knees.

William Cowper (1731–1800)

When I first became the pastor of Westminster Chapel I urged every member to spend thirty minutes a day in quiet time. I thought the chandeliers would crash down! But after they got over the shock of that suggestion, some did seek to spend thirty minutes a day in quiet time (though some didn't). I urge every minister in full-time Christian service to spend an *hour* a day in quiet time (not counting sermon preparation or praying for people). Yet figures show that the average church leader in both the UK and the USA spends four minutes a day in their quiet time. And we wonder why the Church is powerless? But if you were to spend at least half an hour a day in your quiet time you would find yourself knowing what God is like in ever-increasing measure. You would also develop not only knowledge of his ways, but a love for them. And – surprise, surprise – wisdom then sets in.

The consequences

Third, I demonstrate that I choose the fear of the Lord by remembering that there will be a consequence of my decisions. There is a teaching running right through Scripture that many neglect and some are embarrassed about – namely, that God often gets our attention by appealing to our self-interest. For example, Jesus said for us not to judge another or we would be judged. Do you like it when someone judges you – someone who points the finger at you? I certainly don't. Well, Jesus says, 'Do not judge, and you will not be judged' (Luke 6:37). He speaks to our self-interest. Paul said this regarding the matter of giving: '. . . whoever sows generously will also reap generously' (2 Cor. 9:6). Indeed, if we bring all our tithes to the storehouse we will not be able to contain the blessing (Mal. 3:10). Moses made a strategic decision when he refused to be known as the son of Pharaoh's daughter and enjoy the pleasures of this life, but chose instead to be identified with the suffering people of God. Why ever did he do such a thing? Answer: '. . . he was looking ahead to his reward' (Heb. 11:26). It is not wrong to be motivated by reward – Moses was. And if Moses could be motivated in that way, so can I. It is wisdom to be motivated by the consequences of today's decisions.

Life at its longest is still short. Fifty years ago seems like yesterday to me. And as Billy Graham once said, 'The older I get the faster time flies.' It is only a matter of time that we reap what we sow (Gal. 6:7). Tomorrow comes so suddenly with a brutal vehemence that we are stunned. But should we be? If we make the decision not to live for the pleasures of the here and now, but instead for the consequences of right choices, we will be so glad. That day of reaping will come soon.

There are two consequences that will bear our examination.

God's chastening

Apart from reward, there are two other things that should motivate us. The first is the possibility of God disciplining us. Whom the Lord loves he disciplines (Heb. 12:6). It is not a disgrace to be disciplined, or chastened; it shows you are a true child of God. Being disciplined comes from a Greek word that means 'enforced learning'. We are all imperfect, and yet God does not discipline us to 'get even' for some wrongdoing in our past; God 'got even' at the cross: '. . . as far as the east is from the west, so far has he removed our transgressions from us' (Ps. 103:12). And yet God lovingly corrects us when we err, and David is the only person in the Bible called a 'man after his [God's] own heart' (1 Sam. 13:14; Acts 13:22). But the chastening David underwent was extremely hard, and it was precisely because God loved him. And yet it was chastening that could have been avoided had David not given in to sexual temptation (2 Sam. 11).

There are three levels of disciplining: (1) internal – through the Word (the best way to get your problems solved); (2) external – Plan B, when God goes to harsher measures to get our attention (as he did with King David); and (3) terminal chastening – when God says, 'Your time is up', and takes us home (1 Cor. 11:30).

But what does Proverbs 1:26 mean – that God may 'laugh' at us? The worst possible scenario – so easily avoided – is when God 'laughs' at our calamity (Prov. 1:26). This does not mean he laughs in the sense that he is happy or is gloating over our misfortune. No; it grieves him. The reference to God 'laughing' is a figure of speech indicating that God simply will not sympathise, or come to our rescue, after a period of continuously rejecting him.

The judgment seat of Christ

The second consequence we should consider is that *all of us* will one day stand before the judgment seat of Christ. It is when we will give an account of the things done 'while in the body' (2 Cor. 5:10). This refers to what we do in our lifetime – while on earth. Like it or not, you and I will have to stand before our Lord Jesus Christ. Paul uses a Greek word, *bema*, in 2 Corinthians 5:10. You can go to Corinth today and still see the Bema Seat. It was the place in ancient Corinth where rewards and punishments were handed out. Paul did not use a Greek word that simply means 'judgment', although he could have. He used a word that every Corinthian would grasp – namely, that rewards *and* punishments are declared at the Bema Seat.

Therefore choosing the fear of the Lord is to dignify God's wisdom. It is recognising the inevitable consequence of the decision to choose 'the fear of the Lord', and the horrible consequence of not doing so.

The cost of wisdom

Wisdom has a price. It 'costs', say the Proverbs. Wisdom is not purchased with money, but 'costs' means the willingness to abandon certain pleasures of the world, the flesh or the devil. The cost may pertain to our pride. The cost could result in changing our lifestyle or our choice of friends. The cost could be in forfeiting their approval: '. . . get wisdom. Though it *cost all you have*, get understanding' (Prov. 4:7 – my italics). The possibility of a level of wisdom that could dazzle the world is not promised to well-connected people, those with a high profile or great wealth (1 Cor. 1:26). Wisdom is offered to anyone who is willing to put the fear of the Lord first in their lives.

I find this encouraging. As I have said, this means that ordinary people like you and me can attain to the very thing that the ancient Greeks thought was out of reach, or off limits, to nearly everybody. A high IQ is not required – in fact, it may even be a hindrance. Why? Because people with a high IQ can be the hardest to reach, partly because they often assume that logic, or reason, is a superior way of knowing than simple faith in the gospel of Christ. A university degree is not required – and again could even be a barrier. Why? For the same reason. You may have heard the expression 'You can always tell an Oxford man . . . but you can't tell him much.' Being well connected is not required, as people like this often lean on their friends to get jobs and invitations.

But with the pursuit of wisdom one is certainly not reckoning on being born to privilege, or having money or being cultured. This is because the wisdom that we are talking about in this book comes only from *God*. It is his prerogative to give or withhold it. And yet it is promised to those who make a wise choice – to choose to follow his ways.

2

Common Grace

He [your Father in heaven] causes his sun to rise
on the evil and the good, and sends rain on the
righteous and the unrighteous. (Matt. 5:45)

Every good and perfect gift is from above, coming
down from the Father of the heavenly lights, who
does not change like shifting shadows. (Jas. 1:17)

We should take full advantage of those wise people that God places in our paths because we all need good mentors. We also need friends who will lovingly but candidly tell us things we need to hear. You could not begin to grasp how much I am grateful for men like J. I. Packer or Martyn Lloyd-Jones, and I could mention a dozen others that you will never have heard of. These men changed my life and I am so thankful to God for them. I am so blessed.

I was not born to privilege. As some readers will know, I come from Kentucky, and I grew up there in the days when there were only forty-eight states in the USA. Kentucky was forty-seventh in terms of educational standards – which meant we weren't bottom. We had a saying then – 'Thank God for Arkansas', because they were in forty-eighth place! Imagine then how I felt when, in later years, I found myself studying in the Bodleian Library at Oxford alongside students who had been to the top schools in the UK. I never really enjoyed my time at Oxford; for the whole three years, I was too filled with anxiety that I would fail.

My father was a rate clerk with the Chesapeake and Ohio Railway Company in Ashland, Kentucky. He was a man of average intelligence, but he loved God more than anyone I have ever known – the best explanation of why I have had any measure of success. He taught me to be a man of prayer, and this is what has saved me and got me through a liberal seminary which in turn recommended me for Oxford. Without J. I. Packer, probably the most influential evangelical theologian in the world today, I don't think I would have made it through Oxford; and without Dr Lloyd-Jones, the greatest preacher since Charles Spurgeon, I would not have survived twenty-five years at Westminster Chapel.

Dr Lloyd-Jones was one of the most intelligent, and wisest, men I have ever met. His quality of intellect is something that comes around every few hundred years – rather like the Leonardo da Vincis and the Michelangelos of this world. He was both intelligent and intellectual – at home with both the arts and sciences. He read the latest medical journals for light reading. He was also a 'political animal' – he loved politics. Had he gone into politics he would have (in my opinion) become prime minister. The

Reverend Maynard James, the late editor of *Flame* magazine, used to say that Dr Lloyd-Jones had the 'gift of wisdom' – and those who knew the Doctor (as we called him) would agree.

But Dr Lloyd-Jones always made a distinction between being intellectual and being intelligent. He reckoned that a typical cockney taxi driver in London often had more intelligence than an Oxford or Cambridge don. We have all heard of the 'absent-minded professor' – a reference to a very intellectual person but one who is often devoid of common sense. This is what Dr Lloyd-Jones meant by a cockney taxi driver often having more *intelligence* than a university professor. A cockney taxi driver may not have an academic bent, but is 'streetwise' and has discernment or intuition. Intelligence can be gauged by how quickly you catch on rather than how much knowledge you have in your head.

It is certainly true that you can be intellectual but not intelligent. You may be able to read vast amounts of material and remember what you have read. You may be at home with physics, chemistry, languages or literature. But you may also neglect to brush your teeth, shine your shoes, or dress well. You may be an academic capable of winning a Nobel Prize, but lack charm, etiquette or social graces. You may have a high IQ and more than one doctorate – but be so aloof that nobody wants to know you, so conceited that no one enjoys your company, and so arrogant that you have no friends. I know people with both a PhD and an MD who are so rude that those around them feel more contempt than admiration.

What is equally the case, I'm afraid, is that some prestigious people, titled people and those 'born to privilege', are at times neither intellectual nor intelligent. Some are arrogant and believe they have the right to be respected. They are sometimes empty-headed and patronising, speak with posh accents but have little discernment, jump queues in supermarkets because they think they are better than others – not having a clue, or care, as to how they are actually perceived. I remember an Oxford don getting on the same bus with me daily near the Bodleian going to Headington, Oxford (where we lived) whose loud upper-class accent was heard by nearly everybody on the bus. The other passengers would roll their eyes as he spoke; he had no objectivity about himself at all.

What is true, then, is that you can be intellectual and not have wisdom; you can be highly educated and not have wisdom; you can even be intelligent and not have wisdom. Wisdom is not necessarily knowledge. Wisdom is how you *use* the knowledge you have. And in any case, true wisdom comes from the fear of the Lord – the ability to say and do the right thing at the right time. Wisdom is discernment; cutting through the nonsense that most people swallow. Wisdom is far, far greater than having intelligence or being clever.

Exception: 'Special grace in nature'

There is, however, an important exception to what I have said so far about wisdom and the fear of the Lord. There have been those in history – and in my own life – who have demonstrated astonishing wisdom yet may not have known the Lord. I think of people like Sir Winston Churchill, one of the greatest men in human history. He was in some ways to England like Moses was to Israel, especially in the Second World War. For one thing he saw the menace of Adolf Hitler when people like Neville Chamberlain were totally blind to it. But Churchill stuck to his guns, and it is to the glory of God and England that Churchill was able to convince Parliament how evil Hitler in fact was. What a tragedy it would have been had Chamberlain not been found out to be wrong in the nick of time. Churchill was endowed with prodigious wisdom, although I (sadly) know of no evidence that this great man knew the Lord.

What is the explanation? John Calvin called it 'special grace in nature'. It is a case of God graciously endowing people – saved or lost – with specific abilities, gifts or talents. It is usually called *common grace.* This means grace given commonly to all people. 'Common' not because it is ordinary; quite the opposite: it may be indeed extraordinary. But a measure of gifting or wisdom is given commonly to all people in various measures – men and women, saved and lost, educated and uneducated. Not all are movers and shakers, but common grace is showered on all people to some degree.

Here's the crucial principle to grasp: *it is not always easy to discern the difference between what is rooted directly in the wisdom of the Holy Spirit and what can actually be explained by common grace.* The latter can be manifested in a way that would seem to be the exception to the principles of the very wisdom as outlined in this book. Perhaps some of these people are truly converted and regenerated by the Holy Spirit. Who knows for sure? But there is often a cloud of doubt as to whether such people have come to know the Lord. The point is, it doesn't matter – all people are beneficiaries of this special grace in nature; God causes the sun to shine and the rain to fall on the righteous and unrighteous (Matt. 5:45). Again, I think of people with extraordinary foresight – as in the case of Churchill. Utter graciousness – as in the amazing life of Nelson Mandela. Ingenious intellect – as in the case of Albert Einstein. Historic wisdom – as in the case of Abraham Lincoln. Brilliant musicianship as in the Arthur Rubinsteins and Sergei Rachmaninoffs of this world. Brilliant artistry – as in the Michelangelos and da Vincis of this world.

The Good Samaritan

Take Jesus' parable of the good Samaritan (Luke 10:25–37). Here is an example of incredible compassion:

A man was going down from Jerusalem to Jericho, when he was attacked by robbers. They stripped him of his clothes, beat him and went away, leaving him half dead . . . a Samaritan, as he travelled, came where the man was; and when he saw him, he took pity on him. He went to him and bandaged his wounds, pouring on oil and wine. Then he put the man on his own donkey, brought him to an inn and took care of him. The next day he took out two denarii and gave them to the innkeeper. 'Look after him', he said, 'and when I return, I will reimburse you for any extra expense you may have' (Luke 10:30–35).

In this parable Jesus also said that two religious leaders – a priest and a Levite – who were in the stream of God's very covenant people, saw the same injured man. But they ostensibly avoided this man – passing by 'on the other side' so they would not need to get personally involved (vv. 31–32).

The Samaritan's astonishing graciousness and compassion shows that what may often be called 'Christian' virtues were not exhibited by the very ones you would expect to be helpful, but instead demonstrated by one who was not considered a part of the family of God.

What is the explanation? The answer is: common grace, special grace in nature. Such *goodness* therefore may emerge from people outside the covenant of God. Common grace may thus extend beyond the realm of gifts and talents, but also to personal conduct and character. Such exemplary

behaviour can sometimes be seen in non-Christians, but –
sadly – not always be in evidence in Christians.

'Special grace in nature' means God showering both
extraordinary giftedness, but also astonishing virtues, on
people in their natural (unregenerate) state. Some come to
Christ in their lifetimes; others do not. It is God's special
grace to the world. It is what gives us hospitals, doctors and
nurses, firefighters, military leaders. Our heavenly Father
causing his sun to rise on both the evil and the good, and
sending rain on the righteous and the unrighteous, is what
keeps the world from being completely topsy-turvy. Thank
God for the rule of law, for police officers, for medics, archi-
tects, musicians, scientists. It is said that Albert Einstein's
IQ was 212, but there is no indication that he was a born-
again Christian. I love watching Arthur Rubinstein or
Vladimir Horowitz play Rachmaninoff concertos on
YouTube. In fact, I sometimes prefer listening to them than
playing so-called religious music. I can switch off from a
feeling of stress by listening to Yehudi Menuhin play a
Mendelssohn concerto. These men were endowed with
extraordinary common grace – a gift of God for which the
whole world is grateful.

Common grace is not accidental. Special grace does
not come upon men and women by chance. God the
Creator 'from one man' made 'all the nations, that they
should inhabit the whole earth; and he marked out their
appointed times in history and the boundaries of their
lands' (Acts 17:26).

Sometimes, however, God raises up people not only outside the Church, but within the Church, with a high dosage of special grace – people like St Augustine, Athanasius, Anselm, Thomas Aquinas, John Calvin, and Jonathan Edwards. People like this give the Church a sense of glory that otherwise would have passed behind a cloud. We should pray that God will raise up more people like these.

Presence of mind

At our home on Hilton Avenue in Ashland, Kentucky, we grew up next door to a former black slave whose name was Laif Scott. There is no evidence that Laif Scott ever became a Christian. We loved him, and he loved us. He was a wonderful neighbour, but was always 'Mr Scott'. I will never forget one day when he looked into our backyard and saw my mother about to faint as she was hanging out the washing. He shouted to my father – who hadn't noticed it – in the nick of time. My dad ran to her and caught her as she was falling to the ground, saving her from what might have been a very serious accident.

Mr Scott had been given what is often called 'presence of mind' – a phenomenon that sometimes results in unusual strength or wisdom in a time of severe need. Situations like these – where people are given *presence of mind* – are the result solely and entirely of God's goodness at the level of nature where one's faith is not necessarily related.

You will have quickly detected that my own definition of wisdom – the presence of the mind of the Holy Spirit – is derived from the idea of presence of mind. The presence of the mind of the Holy Spirit is granted to the regenerate. But a person who has not been converted could have presence of mind – the ability to think and act quickly in a manner that only God could bring about. The best of human wisdom can sometimes appear to be as great as godly wisdom.

Nelson Mandela

Consider Nelson Mandela. He was (I think) the greatest man who ever lived apart from certain people in the Bible and church history. Some believe he was a born-again Christian; others do not. But when I consider his amazing demonstration of total forgiveness in South Africa – letting even his torturers off the hook and asking everyone to forgive one another – I ask: 'Can anybody show this kind of Christian love without being a Christian?' He was brought up in a Methodist missionary school in South Africa and was definitely taught Christian principles. He called himself a 'Christian', and I believe that he was.

The question is: 'Could special grace in nature produce a Nelson Mandela?' I believe the answer is yes. But I would be less surprised to discover that the Holy Spirit has been within him since childhood when he almost certainly first came to Jesus Christ. God never leaves us, nor forsakes us. I am inclined to think that godly wisdom – not merely common grace – prevailed in the life of Nelson Mandela. Common grace can do that, and the parable of the good Samaritan is proof of that.

So it should not surprise us that our gracious heavenly Father raises up unusual men and women for special times in history, and that they are given the necessary wisdom for their day. This is our Father's world, and he loves and looks after his creation (Heb. 1:3). We must thank God for the unusual people that come along, and pray for more of them. What a tragedy for a nation if there are no leaders with such wisdom. I sometimes fear that there is a vast dearth of greatness in political and religious leadership today. We should pray that God will raise up good and wise men and women – in the Church and in the world – for such a time as this.

Clever, but not wise

One difference between the UK and the USA – two countries 'separated by a common language' (as George Bernard Shaw put it) – is the use of the word 'clever'. In the UK 'clever' refers to being intellectual, having a very sharp mind, inclined towards being an academic. But in the USA 'clever' refers to being sly, cunning and shrewd. What Brits call 'clever' Americans call 'smart'. Brits use the word 'smart' to mean being well dressed! It took me a long time to adjust to the use of various words in the UK.

If Dr Martyn Lloyd-Jones had the gift of wisdom, so too did his beloved wife Bethan. Among our sweetest memories included spending time with Mrs Martyn Lloyd-Jones, particularly after her husband died. When I used to call on Dr Lloyd-Jones every Thursday between 11 a.m. and 1 p.m., she would make us coffee and provide us with Kit Kats, stay a few minutes, then leave us alone. This happened weekly for those four memorable years (1977–81) until the Doctor died. But I kept going to see Mrs Lloyd-Jones for several years, until she too passed away. In my opinion Mrs Lloyd-Jones may have equalled her husband in wisdom – not because she too was a medical doctor, but because she had the wisdom that comes from choosing the fear of the Lord.

One day when I went to see Mrs Lloyd-Jones she had the television on. We watched the prime minister's 'question time' – when MPs put hard questions to the prime minister. I asked Mrs Lloyd-Jones what she thought of the person who was then prime minister. Her reply was: 'Clever, but not wise.' That put it very well. So often we see people in high places who are regarded as having political ingenuity, making brilliant statements and historic pronouncements – but whose judgments are so often wrong. They are clever – maybe even brilliant – but not always very wise.

The Bible is the Holy Spirit's greatest product. It is godly wisdom from Genesis to Revelation. The Holy Spirit wrote the Bible through dedicated men, and all Scripture is

'God-breathed' (2 Tim. 3:16). Holy men of old wrote as they were moved by the Holy Spirit (2 Pet. 1:21). The Holy Spirit used people who made a choice at some point in their lives; they chose the fear of the Lord; they were people who could be trusted. They did not write according to their 'whims' or theological biases; they wrote as they were enabled to write by the immediate and direct power of the Holy Spirit.

Therefore the knowledge found *only* in the Bible – the '*knowledge* of the Holy One' – is what brings the wisdom I hope we can all inherit. It is this very understanding which, sadly, clever people often miss. In other words, true wisdom – taking note of the exception indicated in this chapter – comes to those who *know the Lord*.

Do not lament that you don't have a brain like Albert Einstein or cannot play the piano like Arthur Rubinstein. We should not feel sorry for ourselves if we consider we have not been granted a high level of common grace. Wisdom is demonstrated when we come to terms with the *limits* of our gift, intellect or intelligence. In my book *The Anointing*, I call it 'accepting one's anointing' – especially our limits. I cannot be Jonathan Edwards or Martyn Lloyd-Jones. You may not be a Churchill or an Einstein. But the greatest compensation will be at the judgment seat of Christ where you and I will be judged not by our worldly accomplishments or profile, but whether we chose the fear of the Lord.

As I have shown, the ancient Greeks thought that the greatest philosophical thinkers alone have *sophia* wisdom.

My book is written to encourage the most ordinary person on earth to realise that *sophia* wisdom is on offer to all who choose the fear of the Lord. To know the Lord is to have access to what he has written. His word is a lamp for our feet and a light for our paths (Ps. 119:105). The unfolding of his words gives light (Ps. 119:130). When the Bible is carefully handled, correctly interpreted, fearfully explained – *and sincerely followed* – wisdom sets in.

It is amazing. So whether we are talking about prime ministers, presidents, Nobel Prize winners, Harvard or Oxbridge professors, doctors, lawyers, artists or those people born to privilege, if they do not choose the fear of the Lord they will be devoid of the presence of the mind of the Spirit that you and I can possess.

Another exception

You may want to ask: 'So are brilliant or privileged people ever allowed to have godly wisdom?' Of course they are. It is up to them. Paul made an exception in his comments concerning not many high-powered people being called. Here is the observation that all should heed: 'Not many of you were wise by human standards; not many were influential; not many were of noble birth' (1 Cor. 1:26). Thankfully, Paul did not say 'not *any*' but 'not many'. It just happens, as I said in the previous chapter, that people born to privilege or who have great minds are often the hardest to reach.

They feel that Christianity is 'beneath' them, that they are a cut above those who trust the death of Jesus Christ for their salvation. It is consequently quite rare for a privileged person to come to Christ.

So thank God that there are exceptions. The wisdom to say the right thing at the right time is on offer to everyone – regardless of background or natural ability.

I would hate to be 'clever, but not wise'. If my choice of the fear of the Lord is not applauded or vindicated in this life, who cares? It is *understanding* that I want. I want to understand God's will. I want to grasp God's Word. I want to know his ways. This will absolutely lead me where I should go. I want to make the kind of choice in this world that one day will mean – when I stand before Jesus Christ himself – that he will look right into my eyes and say 'Well done'. I want that more than anything in the world. What is more, the judgment seat of Christ will be the vindication of true wisdom.

3

A Secret

The secret of the LORD is with them
that fear him; and he will shew them
his covenant. (Ps. 25:14, AV)

'What no eye has seen, what no ear has heard,
and what no human mind has conceived' –
the things God has prepared for those who
love him – these are the things that God has
revealed to us by his Spirit. (1 Cor. 2:9–10)

Recently when using my computer I put on my earphones to listen to music so it didn't bother anybody else in the room. Yet again I was enjoying Arthur Rubinstein playing Rachmaninoff's Concerto No. 2 in C Minor for piano and orchestra – probably my favourite piece of music. Suddenly the music stopped, so I changed the batteries in my earphones. I still couldn't hear any music – only when I disconnected the earphones, when *everybody* in the room could hear it! I tried a different set of earphones. Still no music through the earphones. I tried everything I knew to make things work. It seemed something had happened to my computer. I would need to take it into the Apple store. I hated the thought of being without my music, especially when flying on my next trip. I phoned our son T.R. to tell him about my problem, and he asked if my finger had accidentally touched the mute key on my keyboard. So I then pushed the mute key – and the music returned! One little touch of my finger on the right key and the music continued as before. I had envisaged having to buy a new computer or to wait for days to get it repaired. No repairer would have found the solution if he had taken the whole computer apart. All it needed was touching the right key on my keyboard. Simple as that.

Wisdom is a secret. God alone holds the key to it. If he gives us the key, wisdom comes. If he doesn't give us the key, no amount of agony, time, panic, earnest searching, twisting his arm or effort on our part will bring about the wisdom we want. God holds the key, and one little touch from him and the secret is unlocked. It is so simple; so easy for him to do – but totally hidden from us until God steps in.

Only God knows what is truly best for us, and *wants* what is best for us (Ps. 84:11). He knows what we should do; what we should say; how we should plan; whom we need to meet; where we should go; what is our responsibility; our calling; our future. God knows the exact time when we should speak or act. He knows the end from the beginning; he knows the future as perfectly as he knows the past (Isa. 46:10). Because he only wants what is best for us, he knows the exact pitfalls we should avoid. If we get the mind of the Holy Spirit we can avoid unnecessary mistakes. We are therefore utterly dependent on him to reveal to us what it is we should say and do. Apart from God imparting wisdom to us, the best you and I can do is to speculate. But the best speculation is not good enough. His wisdom is not a leap in the dark; it is walking in the light.

God can give or withhold mercy and, either way, still be equally fair with us and true to himself (Rom. 9:15). So too with wisdom; he can give it or withhold it and be totally just either way.

What is the point of this? It is that the sovereignty of God should teach us that we can never graduate to a position whereby we are now qualified to *demand* wisdom. We can only ask (Jas. 1:5). Even if we are faithful in all his commands, we cannot snap our fingers at him and expect him to jump at our request. What if we are obedient in resisting the temptations relative to money, sex or power? Answer: we never get upgraded to the status of entitlement. We are only doing our 'duty' (Luke 17:10).

We live in a heartless, cruel world in which being well connected can get certain people to the place they want to be; this largely depends on who they know and how much money they have. In such cases, then, 'money is the answer for everything' (Eccles. 10:19). If you have enough money you can live in the best location, enjoy the best foods, travel the world. You can pay for a first-class ticket and then are entitled to a more comfortable seat. There are those who never want for anything when it comes to material things; such people are excessively wealthy and are *used to* being entitled to things. They simply pay for them.

But wisdom is not for sale. Even if I have done all that is required of me, I am still never – ever – in a position to say, 'Look here, God, I have done what you told me to do, now hand over your wisdom.' No, it is not like that.

Wisdom is a gift. If we had earned it, wisdom would be like God paying our salary. In such a case we would be entitled to it. But the mind of the Spirit is what God grants graciously, and it is known only to God. His giving us the presence of his mind is a gift more precious than gold – something money cannot buy. And yet this wisdom is a secret that God can unlock or keep hidden – and still be just either way.

All we can do is ask. Wisdom will lead you to go to him on bended knee and ask for mercy (Heb. 4:16). Never fall into the counterproductive trap of thinking you deserve something good from God. It is the devil – who loves to accuse God – who will make you think God owes you good things.

God can keep a secret

Not many people can keep a secret. Many of us might *claim* to be able to keep a secret, but if it is something that will bolster our self-esteem – even if we were so sure originally we wouldn't tell – not all of us can manage to keep that secret. Could you have tea with the Queen and keep quiet about it? Could I have met Nelson Mandela and never told someone about it? Do you know anybody who can hold some very interesting information inside and never tell it? If so, that is a rare person.

But God can keep a secret. You could almost say that keeping a secret is what he does best. For example, the best-kept secret from the foundation of the world was his reason for sending his Son into the world. No one knew – neither Satan nor the angels – that Jesus Christ the eternal Son of God would die on a cross for the sins of the world to satisfy the justice and wrath of God. Not even the prophets *fully* perceived what they accurately foretold. It wasn't even grasped by his disciples – who saw the resurrected Jesus with their very eyes – until the Holy Spirit came upon them on the Day of Pentecost. It was then – and not until then – that things 'came together' for them. The Holy Spirit – the Second Person of the Trinity – unveiled the secret (Acts 2:1–36) because the Holy Spirit knows the 'deep things of God' (1 Cor. 2:10).

Do you think the devil knows the future? He knows *only* what God lets him in on. For example, he has been given a glimpse of his ultimate demise. The demons recognised who Jesus was and in doing so revealed they knew of their end. 'What do you want with us, Son of God?' they shouted. 'Have you come here to torture us before the appointed time?' (Matt. 8:29). The devil knows that his time is short (Rev. 12:10). And though the demons knew who Jesus was they had no idea that his crucifixion – which they thought was their own idea – guaranteed their destruction. Had they known this, 'they would not have crucified the Lord of glory' (1 Cor. 2:8). In other words, it was a secret known only to God and totally hidden from Satan.

Another example of a secret that God keeps is the way he will clear his name one day. Yes. He will clear his Name. You may say: 'God has a lot to answer for – allowing the evil and suffering in the world which he could stop in one stroke.' I would reply: '[The day will come] when every knee will bow . . . and every tongue acknowledge that Jesus Christ is Lord, to the glory of God the Father' (Phil. 2:9–11). As I show in my book *Totally Forgiving God*, he will clear his name in such a way, and with such integrity, that no one – nobody – will say, 'This is not fair.'

Yes, God can keep a secret. So no effort to coerce him, no bribe, no promise of what we will do, or getting the holiest saint to intercede for you, will persuade him to reveal what he has chosen to keep secret. The greatest brain cannot break the code. The most worthy person, the most famous, the one who has suffered the most, or the person who has prayed the longest, cannot make God impart his wisdom.

The secret of wisdom is on offer

But he has *chosen* to reveal that secret to those who fear him, and only them. 'The secret of the LORD is with them that fear him' (Ps. 25:14, AV). In other words, this secret is unveiled to that person – however bright or however simple

– who chooses the fear of the Lord. While the greatest mind will try to display brilliance, ingenuity and wisdom in showing what will solve a problem – but fail – the simplest mind is told to jump the queue and be given the things of the Spirit of God that bypass the so-called wise and prudent. On one occasion Jesus lifted up his eyes heavenwards and actually said, 'I praise you, Father, Lord of heaven and earth, because you have *hidden these things from the wise and learned*, and revealed them to little children. Yes, Father, for this is what you were pleased to do' (Matt. 11:25–26 – my italics).

The result of God hiding things from the wise and learned is – in effect – a type of blindness. God can keep you from seeing what is there – even if it is before your very eyes. There are many stories of people taking Bibles into the old Soviet Union and China when the border authorities did not even notice them! The two men on the road to Emmaus were 'kept' from seeing Jesus (Luke 24:16). The Holy Spirit kept these two men 'blind' until the moment God chose for them to recognise him. But at the chosen moment 'their eyes were opened and they recognised him' (Luke 24:31).

The people of Israel by and large have been inflicted with a similar blindness. In my book with Rabbi David Rosen (*The Christian and the Pharisee*), I said that there is even a 'double blindness' on Israel. First, *all* people are blind already from seeing the light of the knowledge of the glory of God in Jesus' face because the god of this world – Satan – has done it (2 Cor. 4:4). But in addition to this, God has given to Israel 'a spirit of stupor, eyes that could not see and ears that could not hear' (Rom. 11:8). If you wonder why it is so hard to reach a Jew with the gospel of Jesus Christ, this is why. There are exceptions, thank God. But sadly, so far, they are few.

But one day – may it come soon – that blindness will be lifted and it will be as easy to reach a Jew for Jesus as eating strawberries and cream at Wimbledon. God will determine that day.

We must never forget the sovereignty of God. In the same way that you did not snap your fingers at God when you came to him to be saved, but you asked for mercy, so you keep asking for mercy when you approach him. I fear that many forget this, but even the most mature Christian never outgrows asking God for mercy. 'Let us then approach God's throne of grace with confidence, so *that we may receive mercy* and find grace to help us in our time of need' (Heb. 4:16 – my italics). This is a verse written for Christians! In other words, the first thing we are to ask for when we pray is mercy.

This is especially apt when it comes to wisdom. Knowing that wisdom is God's secret, we dare not approach him with a haughty spirit – as if he owes us something. If you *do* feel he owes you something, I would lovingly question whether you are saved! Never imagine that God owes you anything; this is why we ask for mercy.

So if it is wisdom you want – and since God alone holds the key to this wisdom – you and I must go to him on bended knee. This shows we have a proper fear of him. The secret of the Lord is with them that fear him. You respect him. You are in awe of him. You therefore ask for mercy that you might find grace for wisdom in your time of need.

A difficult scripture

But what about asking for wisdom in faith *without any doubting*? That is what James said. First, he said that if any of us lacks wisdom we should simply ask God. I welcome that. James added that God gives this generously 'without finding fault, and it will be given to you' (Jas. 1:5). I like that a lot too. So far, so good. But James added something that gives me a sinking feeling; I almost wish he hadn't said it: 'But when you ask, you must *believe and not doubt*, because the one who doubts is like a wave of the sea, blown and tossed by the wind. That person should not expect to receive anything from the Lord. Such a person is double-minded and unstable in all they do' (vv. 6–8 – my italics). Oh dear – this means I should not expect anything, and also that I am double-minded and unstable, because I have to be honest and admit that I have asked God for wisdom many times and doubted many times.

This is not so easy to explain. First, I am not sure how many people pray without ever doubting – surely only Jesus prayed without ever doubting? He alone had the Holy Spirit without any limit (John 3:34). What James puts before us is virtually the same thing as Jesus puts before us. He said,

'. . . if anyone says to this mountain, "Go, throw yourself into the sea," and does not doubt in their heart but believes that what they say will happen, it will be done for them' (Mark 11:23). True. But – apart from an allegorical interpretation of Mark 11:23 – how many people have literally prayed for a mountain to be removed and for it to disappear before their very eyes? I haven't. But there is no doubt that if I truly prayed with that kind of faith, such a mountain would disappear before my eyes.

In a similar way James, who challenges us to pray without doubting, also said that the prayer of faith will save the sick (Jas. 5:15). I have prayed for people with physical needs hundreds of times, but the truth is that I have not seen a lot of them healed – though I have seen *some* of them miraculously healed. But I have never *consciously* prayed the prayer of faith a single time that I am aware of – as if I knew immediately that the person would be healed. This has not happened in my own experience. And yet – because I know people have been healed through my praying for them – I know that the conscious prayer of faith is not an absolute prerequisite for people to be healed.

James did not say that a person who doubts won't have his or her prayers answered. He said that the person who doubts should not *expect* to have those prayers answered. We may not have the expectancy, but God is greater than our expectancy. He may choose to answer our prayer because we *asked* – not because we prayed without doubting. Behind all our praying with a limited faith is our Great

High Priest who intercedes for us at God's right hand with a perfect faith. That is why our prayers are answered. It is Jesus' faith that lies behind answered prayer. If it wasn't, you and I would begin to take ourselves too seriously.

In the exact same way, then, I pray for wisdom – all the time. I can't say, though, that I pray without doubting. I simply ask. And guess what! I have been given wisdom when I needed it countless times. I therefore do not take James' challenge to believe 'and not doubt' as an absolute requirement to receiving wisdom. Otherwise, if I am to be totally honest, I don't think I would ever have been given wisdom. I am therefore not discouraged when I ask for wisdom and don't have perfect faith.

The same is true when it comes to praying in the will of God. In order to be heard, we must pray in God's will for that is the way we are 'heard'. But if we '*know* that he hears us – whatever we ask – we know that we *have* what we asked of him' (1 John 5:14–15 – my italics). We have two things here: (1) praying in the will of God, and (2) knowing you pray in his will. If the latter is the case with you, you are assured your prayer will be answered. But does it follow that if we *don't* know we have been heard, our prayer cannot be answered? No. The proof of this is the prayer of Zechariah who prayed for a son, but after a while gave up praying for this. Then one day the angel Gabriel announced to Zechariah, '. . . your prayer has been heard' (Luke 1:13). Zechariah didn't believe it! But his prayer was none the less answered and John the Baptist was born. Zechariah's unbelief did not stop his prayer being answered. This is because any prayer prayed in the will of God – whether we consciously pray in his will or not – will be answered.

So do not be overly concerned if you don't pray in perfect faith, or know for sure that you prayed in God's will.

So what do I do? I know that God holds the key and that he knows the next step forward. The Holy Spirit *always* knows what to do next. I simply say, 'Lord, I come to you to ask for mercy, that I might find wisdom in this hour – to know what to do now.' That's it. That is exactly how I pray. And although I cannot say God answers me as I wish every single time that I pray, he does answer me at times. That's good enough for me.

One last thing. God delights in mercy, and loves to show mercy. He is a merciful God. He knows our frame, remembers that we are dust (Ps. 103:14). Psalm 103:14 is possibly my favourite verse in all the psalms. It coheres with Hebrews 4:15 – that our Great High Priest is sympathetic with our weaknesses. So when we pray we should remember to begin by asking for 'mercy', as the writer says in Hebrews 4:16. As we have seen, God can give mercy or withhold it, and be just either way. Likewise God can give faith or withhold it – lest we begin to take ourselves too seriously.

Go to your heavenly Father and ask. He has the key. He can unlock your mind; take the dimness from your eyes; increase your ability to hear; and give you wisdom that defies a natural explanation – in one second. Just ask.

The unveiling of the secret is not far away.

4

An Invitation You Cannot Refuse

> If you are pleased with me, teach me your
> ways so I may know you and continue to
> find favour with you. (Exod. 33:12-13)

> 'Ask for whatever you want me to give
> you.' Solomon answered ... '... give your
> servant a discerning heart to govern
> your people and to distinguish between
> right and wrong.' (1 Kings 3:5-6, 9)

Have you ever fantasised that God might come to you –
as he did to Moses and Solomon – and make you a
proposition: ask for anything you want and you shall have
it? I have. I have also asked myself, 'What would I have said
to God had he come to me as he did to Solomon?' Would I
have asked for wisdom – or something else?

So what would *you* say to God if he said to you, 'What
do you want me to do for you?' That is what Jesus said to a
blind man. The man understandably replied, 'Lord, I want
to see.' Jesus healed him then and there (Luke 18:41–42).

I have frequently asked people the question, 'If you could have anything you want from God, and knew he would give it, what would you ask for?' I have had answers that ranged from 'win the lottery', to 'good health', to 'financial success', to 'that my loved one will be saved'.

So what would you ask the Lord to do – if you knew in advance that you were absolutely and unequivocally going to get it? One thing is certain, it would surely be an offer you could not refuse!

Over the years when I have come to 1 Kings 3 in my Bible reading plan – and read the account of God offering Solomon *carte blanche* – I have written in the margin of my Bible what *I* would say to God. It is not always the same; it varies from year to year. I try to envisage God's proposition had I not known about Solomon's response.

Two kinds of wisdom

The two scenarios regarding Moses and Solomon are similar. Each of them could ask God for anything – and get what they wanted. And although their answers were pleasing to God, there is a subtle difference between them. Moses' request was to know God's ways in order to maintain divine favour; Solomon's was to discern between right and wrong in governing the people of Israel.

Why is this comparison important? Because it shows two kinds of wisdom: (1) theological wisdom – that of Moses;

and (2) practical wisdom – what Solomon was given. Both of these are needed. When these two kinds of wisdom are found simultaneously in the body of Christ it is a wonderful thing. In 1 Corinthians 12 Paul discusses spiritual gifts in the body of Christ, and makes it clear that there needs to be a variety of gifts and callings in the Church. He asks: 'If the whole body were an eye, where would the sense of hearing be? If the whole body were an ear, where would the sense of smell be? But in fact God has arranged the parts in the body, every one of them, just as he wanted them to be. If they were all one part, where would the body be? As it is, there are many parts, but one body' (1 Cor. 12:17–20).

Theological wisdom

Theological wisdom pertains to the knowledge of the Word and ways of God. Moses asked to know God's 'ways'. He already knew a lot of about God's Word. After all, the Law delivered on Mount Sinai (Exod. 20) was a revelation of God's Word. Both Moses and Solomon asked for what they already had in measure. As for Solomon's request, he demonstrated wisdom in asking for wisdom – as one of our previously suggested definitions of wisdom showed. As for Moses' request, he knew more about God's Word than anybody alive. He had been given the Ten Commandments (which we call the Moral Law), information on how the people of God should worship (Ceremonial Law), and guidance on how they should govern themselves (Civil Law).

'Nearly all the wisdom we possess, that is to say, true and sound wisdom, consists of two parts,' said John Calvin in his opening statement in *Institutes of the Christian Religion*, 'the knowledge of God and of ourselves.' The knowledge of God refers to what God is in himself – his character, his being, his attributes. In the unveiling of the Ten Commandments comes the knowledge of righteousness and sin. Because God is a jealous God he will not abide his people having any other god before him (Exod. 20:3; Exod. 34:14). God outlawed murder, adultery, stealing – even coveting (Exod. 20:13–17).

In the unfolding of the Ceremonial Law comes the knowledge of God's justice with regard to sin. The sacrificial system further demonstrates God's hatred for sin and the need for atonement through the shedding of blood: '. . . it is the blood that makes atonement for one's life' (Lev. 17:11). Such sacrifices, however, were but a 'shadow' of things that would come (Heb. 10:1) – the reality being the person of Jesus Christ shedding his blood for our sins (Heb. 9:12). The Civil Law shows how the Israelites should govern themselves, the need to get along with one another, and how they must face the consequence of injustice. What Paul called the 'law of Christ' (1 Cor. 9:21; Gal. 6:2) is unfolded in forgiveness towards one another (Eph. 4:32).

And yet when Moses asked to know God's *ways* it suggests that the Law that had been given to him did not in and of itself satisfy Moses' yearning to know God as he desired. Moses wanted more of what he had already. It is like Paul's yearning 'to know Christ' (Phil. 3:10). Of course

Paul knew the Lord – but he wanted more. And that is what was at bottom in Moses' request to God in Exodus 33:13. Moses felt that he did not know God himself well. He did not know enough of God's ways to be to the Israelites what they needed. This is why – when given an opportunity to ask for anything – Moses asked, 'Teach me your ways'.

I will never forget when I 'saw' this for the first time – that is, when it first gripped me. I must have read this verse hundreds of times, but for some reason as I read Exodus 33:13 one day I was convicted. Moses could have had anything under the sun that day. But what did he ask for? To be taught God's ways. Amazing. He knew God's ways more than anybody – ever. But he felt he did not know God's ways enough. What convicted me was that I knew in my heart that this request of Moses is *not* what I would have asked for. I would probably have asked for a double anointing, taking my cue from Isaiah 61:7 ('you will receive a double portion') and 2 Kings 2:9 (Elisha's request for a 'double portion' of Elijah's spirit). Whereas Moses' request was God-centred, mine was largely self-centred. It made me see how Moses was so honoured of God. Exodus 33:13 revealed the real Moses. I think an invitation to ask for 'anything' reveals our character like nothing else could – it unveils the real you. Moses' request shows the kind of man that God had chosen to lead the ancient people of Israel.

How many people are like Moses?

John Calvin also noted that true wisdom consists of 'knowledge of ourselves'. For true theological knowledge is to show us what we are like – including our *sin*. So much 'wisdom' that is on offer in so many places today bypasses the most salient fact of all about men and women: we are sinners. Modern psychology, philosophy, sociology, education and economics, speaking generally, do not have humankind's sinful nature on their radar screen. It is the same with some preaching. When we talk about the 'power of positive thinking', 'possibility thinking' and 'feel-good teaching' in some parts of the Church, or even Dale Carnegie's *How to Win Friends and Influence People* (a book I *do* recommend, by the way), the notion of our sin is almost entirely swept under the carpet. You and I will never – ever – get very acquainted with God's ways until we come face to face with our sin. If we say we have no sin, we 'deceive ourselves' and the truth is not in us (1 John 1:8). When Isaiah had a glimpse of the glory of God he instantly became conscious of his own sin (Isa. 6:5).

Practical wisdom

Solomon's request – wisdom to discern right from wrong – is a request largely for practical wisdom. He wanted guidance in getting it right in governing his people. Practical wisdom is utilitarian wisdom; functional wisdom; pragmatic wisdom. The kind of wisdom mostly seen in Proverbs and Ecclesiastes is practical wisdom, but take this caution: do not forget its connection to choosing the fear of God. I would have thought that a person with a proper fear of God who reads *How to Win Friends and Influence People* would get more benefit than anybody.

As I said above, Solomon's request for wisdom showed that he already had wisdom. Can you ever have enough wisdom? There are two close friends – ministerial colleagues – I have prayed for daily for years. These are high-profile men who have shown remarkable wisdom to get to where they are. What do you suppose each of them asks me specifically to pray for when I pray for them? Wisdom and discernment. Solomon had sufficient discernment already to know what was valuable and needed. Where did he get that desire? God put it there. 'Take delight in the LORD and he will give you the desires of your heart' (Ps. 37:4). Solomon's request revealed that there was a good relationship with God in play which preceded his request.

Did God answer Solomon's request? First, God was so pleased with Solomon's desire that he said to him:

> Since you have asked for this and not for long life or wealth for yourself, nor have asked for the death of your enemies but for discernment in administering justice, I will do what you have asked. I will give you a wise and discerning heart, so that there will never have been anyone like you, nor will there ever be. Moreover, I will give you what you have not asked for – both wealth and honour – so that in your lifetime you will have no equal among kings (1 Kings 3:11–13).

When God said to Solomon, 'I will give you what you have not asked for', namely, 'wealth and honour', I think of

Jesus' promise in Matthew 6:33 – my dad's favourite verse: 'But seek ye first the kingdom of God and his righteousness; and all these things will be added unto you' (AV). 'These things' referred to earthly security – food, shelter and clothing. Jesus said we should not worry about the essentials of life – such things are God's responsibility: ' . . . do not worry about your life, what you will eat or drink; or about your body, what you will wear' (Matt. 6:25). Our job is to seek first God's kingdom; his task is to supply our need and, if he wills, see that we have what we didn't ask for! I think this is a message that those who focus on a 'prosperity gospel' need to remember. We should not seek material things, but God's kingdom. If we seek it, we will have all we need. Solomon discovered that by seeking wisdom he got a lot more than he ever envisaged. Or, as C. S. Lewis put it, 'Aim at heaven and you get the earth thrown in; aim at earth and you get neither.'

There was immediate evidence of Solomon's request having been granted. Two prostitutes came to him. They lived in the same house. Each of them had babies, but one of the babies died. The mother of the dead baby stole the living baby and put the dead baby in its place. Therefore both claimed that the living baby was theirs. Solomon knew a way to expose who was lying and find out who was the real mother: 'Bring me a sword . . . Cut the living child in two and give half to one and half to the other.' The real mother cried out, 'Please, my Lord, give her the living baby! Don't kill him!' The other prostitute said, 'Neither I nor you shall have him. Cut him in two!' Solomon's judgment was: 'Give the living baby to the first woman. Do not kill him; she is his mother.' When all Israel heard the verdict the king had given, 'they held the king in awe, because they saw that he had wisdom from God to administer justice' (1 Kings 3:16–28).

The whole world sought out Solomon's wisdom (1 Kings 10:24). The queen of Sheba came to meet him – to test him 'with hard questions'. He answered all of them; '. . . nothing was too hard for the king to explain to her' (1 Kings 10:1, 3).

And yet neither Moses nor Solomon was perfect. Solomon's kingship ended under a cloud. As for Moses, he grieved the Lord by not carrying out the order to 'speak to the rock' to get water instead of striking it – which Moses did twice. The Lord said, 'Because you did not trust in me enough to honour me as holy in the sight of the Israelites, you will not bring this community into the land I give them' (Num. 20:12). Moses was not allowed to enter the Promised Land, and only saw it from a distance. But his stature was so great that God himself buried Moses so that no one would be able to worship at his grave.

Moses and Solomon were referred to in the New Testament with the greatest deference and respect. The apostle John contrasted Moses with Jesus Christ: 'For the law was given through Moses; grace and truth came through Jesus Christ' (John 1:17). Jesus mentioned Solomon twice. First, in the Sermon on the Mount: 'Yet I tell you that not even Solomon in all his splendour was dressed like one of these [lilies in the field]' (Matt. 6:29). Jesus even compared himself to Solomon: 'The Queen of the South will rise at the judgment with the people of this generation and condemn them, for she came from the ends of the earth to listen to Solomon's wisdom, and now something greater than Solomon is here' (Luke 11:31). Moses appeared with Elijah when Jesus was transfigured (Matt. 17:3). Moses' stature was summarised in this way: '. . . no prophet has risen in Israel like Moses, whom the LORD knew face to face . . . For no one has ever shown the mighty power or performed the awesome deeds that Moses did in the sight of all Israel' (Deut. 34:10, 12). Although Solomon's temple had been destroyed hundreds of years before, what remained of it was still called 'Solomon's Colonnade' (John 10:23; Acts 3:11; 5:12).

These two men who were given an invitation they could not refuse made the right choice. Moses and Solomon were men with unparalleled wisdom. No wonder then that those who choose the fear of the Lord are exalted and honoured as they were. As we have already seen, wisdom means they would be given a garland to grace their heads; they would be – and were – crowned with splendour (Prov. 4:9). A good name is to be chosen more than great riches (Prov. 22:1). A good name comes from making wisdom one's choice; wisdom is more precious than gold or rubies (Prov. 8:10–11).

That said, there are worldly invitations that come to people – that sometimes appear too good to turn down. Such invitations may pertain to money, meeting an important person, fame, a chance to win political office, or attaining power and authority. Irresistible invitations? Yes. But are these invitations right to accept simply because you say, 'It was an invitation I could not refuse'? This is a pretty solemn reminder that if we are given an invitation here on earth that we feel we cannot refuse, we should ask whether such an invitation is worth it before we accept.

So if you could have anything you want, what would you choose?

When our prayer request pleases God

There are at least four prayers you can pray and be sure that you are pleasing God with them:

(1) When you ask for wisdom. Solomon's request is proof of that. Also, James 1:5 – inviting us to ask for wisdom – is further proof that asking for wisdom is always acceptable.

(2) When you pray in the will of God. If you pray in God's will you know you have been 'heard'. If you *know* you have been heard, you know in advance you will receive what you asked for (1 John 5:14–15).

(3) Praying with 'groans that words cannot express' since the Sprit intercedes for us according to the will of God (Rom. 8:26–27). I happen to believe

this implicitly refers to praying in tongues since it coheres with 1 Corinthians 14:2: 'For anyone who speaks in a tongue does not speak to people but to God. Indeed, no one understands them; they utter mysteries by the Spirit.'

(4) The Lord's Prayer. Jesus wrote it and told us to pray it (Matt. 6:9–13; Luke 11:2–4).

The essential ingredient in prayer is to pray in the will of God. In other words, if you want to be 'heard' – that is, have your prayer answered – you must pray in God's will. It is when we ask according to his will that God 'hears us' (1 John 5:14).

Praying for wisdom, then, is to pray in the will of God. Would you honestly want what God did not want you to have? God only wants what is best for us. It is in our supreme interest to find out what he wants for us.

God has a plan for your life. Imagine this: you have a plan for your life – and you mapped it out in your own mind, or wrote it down. I guarantee that it would not be as good as what God himself wants for you. You could not improve on what God wants for you if you had a thousand years to work on it. Here is my wisdom for you: ask for God's wisdom.

God loved it when Solomon asked for wisdom. He loves it when you and I do as well.

5

The Prize

... get wisdom. Though it cost all you
have, get understanding. (Prov. 4:7)

... with all thy getting get
understanding. (Prov. 4:7, AV)

Do you not know that in a race all the
runners run, but only one gets the prize?
Run in such a way as to get the prize.
Everyone who competes in the games goes
into strict training. (1 Cor. 9:24–25)

When you read through the book of Proverbs you might get the impression that the various references to wisdom try to outdo one another in showing how important and valuable godly wisdom is – more precious than gold, or rubies. Get wisdom and you will wear a garland. You will have a good name. You will be rewarded beyond your wildest dreams.

As I mentioned earlier, the Hebrew word *biynah* in Proverbs 4:7 is open to more than one accurate translation. It may be translated as 'understanding' or 'insight' – possibly also 'discernment' or 'comprehension' (Amplified Bible). The point is, there is simply nothing greater than wisdom. Get it and you will be rewarded no end. For wisdom is priceless – 'Whatever you get, get insight'. Just get it! Do not settle for second best or Plan B. Whatever it takes, get it!

Vince Lombardi is widely regarded as the greatest coach in American football history. When asked what his secret was, he replied: 'Winning isn't the main thing; it is the only thing.' It is as if Proverbs 4:7 is saying, 'Wisdom – whether you call it understanding or insight – isn't the main thing; it is the *only* thing.'

Insight means the ability to discern the true nature of something. It gets to the heart of the matter and unravels a complicated problem. In the same way that a breakthrough may come suddenly, so with insight; it may be like an epiphany. Insight is an objectively accurate and deeply intuitive understanding of a person or thing. For a doctor, it means a correct diagnosis. For a theologian, it means a true understanding of Christian doctrine or seeing the meaning of an obscure verse in the Bible. For a police officer or detective, it is finding the clue that will solve a difficult crime.

The emphasis in Proverbs is about achieving wisdom, insight or understanding. There are no boundaries suggested. Such understanding is not narrowed down to biblical insight, important though this is to someone like me. *Anybody* can claim the right to insight in Proverbs, whatever line of work they may have. The scientist, the doctor, the economist – such people not only have a right to elbow in on Proverbs, but they are invited to test the waters and discover what the fear of the Lord will bring them.

The urgency and priority of obtaining insight can be summarised in two words: *get it*. Whatever it takes, get it! Get it 'though it cost all you have' (NIV).

Someone might argue that the wisdom of Proverbs is off limits for the politician, doctor or police detective as it is largely about godly wisdom. But this is not a valid view-point because the *only* kind of true wisdom is godly wisdom. There is no other kind. True wisdom comes only from God; he knows everything. So if scientists, politicians or economists are willing to humble themselves, and admit to their lack of insight, all that Proverbs promises is offered to them. When James says if *anyone* lacks wisdom let them ask God (Jas. 1:5); it is an invitation for any person to acknowledge that *all wisdom is in God alone*. He holds the key. After all, '[in Christ] are hidden *all* the treasures of wisdom and knowledge' (Col. 2:3 – my italics).

As the fear of the Lord is the beginning of true wisdom, any doctor, lawyer, architect, scientist, detective or politi-cian shows his or her folly by dismissing the fear of the Lord in his or her life. Notwithstanding the realm of common grace which (as we saw) explains extraordinary knowledge in non-Christians, I believe that countless brilliant and ingenious people have forfeited knowledge that could be theirs by not putting God first in their lives. I invite any gifted person – whatever your calling – to find out for yourself what insight pertaining to the knowledge of your own profession you have been forfeiting by not making the fear of the Lord paramount in your life. If common grace can extend to a non-Christian – and bless people generally – how much more would godly wisdom transform society by a person who is willing to acknowledge that Jesus Christ is Lord.

So if you are in one of these professions or similar, may I ask you something: 'What kind of private devotional life do you have? How much quiet time do you give God? How much do you pray? How well do you know the Bible?' If you make your quiet time a priority – giving it the same attention you would to your appointments at work – I guarantee that there will follow in your life a surprising emergence of wisdom. The day will come when you will cherish your quiet time above all other appointments of your day.

Many years ago Dr Russell V. DeLong (1901–81) wrote a book entitled *The High Cost of Low Living*. In a sense the title speaks for itself – living a life of debauchery takes its toll on one's self-esteem, health, mental acumen, finances, usefulness and general happiness. Likewise, the cost of a lifestyle without self-discipline means the forfeiture of wisdom. We have seen that true wisdom does not necessarily come from being very intelligent, having had a further education, knowledge of culture or even years of experience. It is, though, inseparably connected to the fear of the Lord, and begins with it (Prov. 1:7).

Wisdom is on offer to all of us and is therefore *the prize* one should seek. Go for it – and get it! Paul compares the Christian life to the Olympic Games, a subject with which every Corinthian would have been very familiar. Winning the gold medal is an honour that only comes to one person, however. All runners run in a race, 'but only one gets the prize' (1 Cor. 9:24). And what do they do to win that prize? They go into 'strict training' (1 Cor. 9:25). The self-discipline for the athlete who wins the gold medal is most amazing – extraordinary in fact. I have watched a number of the Olympic gold medallists being interviewed over the years. These men and women discipline their bodies several hours every day – day after day – for years. A gold medal is not won by hard training for a few months prior to the event. It takes years. Few care to 'go there', as the effort isn't worth it for most people.

But there is a crucial difference between the Christian life and the Olympics. With the games 'only one wins the prize'. This is because they are in competition with one another. But in the Christian life *all* of us can win the prize. We are not in competition with one another. Our eyes are fixed on Jesus. He looks at each of us individually – as if there were no one else. Men and women look at the outward appearance; God looks on the heart (1 Sam. 16:7).

Inheritance

All of us can win the prize because each of us has been called to enter into his or her inheritance. Salvation is a free gift of God. We get to heaven by saving faith – transferring our hope in good works to the blood of Jesus Christ. This is called salvation. But there is something that accompanies salvation (Heb. 6:9): inheritance. It is what you get by persistent faith and the pursuit of wisdom. When we have received Christ Jesus the Lord, we need to walk in him (Col. 2:6). Persistent faith will lead us simultaneously to pursue wisdom and come into our inheritance. It is on offer to every believer. Paul calls it 'the prize'. We achieve our reward at the judgment seat of Christ by entering into our inheritance here on earth. Paul was not the slightest bit worried as to whether he would make it to heaven, but he was very concerned indeed that he might be 'disqualified for the prize'. That is why he underwent strict training – 'I strike a blow to my body and make it my slave' (1 Cor. 9:27).

The word 'inheritance' can be used interchangeably with 'prize', 'crown' or 'reward'. So how do we get this prize? By persistent faith and pursuing wisdom. Making wisdom our priority guarantees we will come into our inheritance.

'Inheritance' is to be understood in two ways: internal and external. 'Internal' refers to our pursuit of wisdom; making it our priority; walking in the light; following

Scripture; keeping our eyes on Jesus; resisting the temptations that deter us from our goal. These things are 'internal' – the priority of the mind, the desire of the heart, and the exercise of the will.

'External' inheritance, however, refers to your calling in life: your gifting, ability, job, position. External inheritance refers to your profile, your degree of success.

God chose our inheritance for us (Ps. 47:5) and this means what he has planned for us is out of our hands. He does not consult us – we consult him and find out what it is he wants us to do.

Caution: it needs to be internal first, then external. We need to get the right order. In other words, don't ask, 'What is my external inheritance?' Ask, 'Am I pursuing wisdom? Is God's will for me my priority? Am I keeping my eyes on Jesus?'

Get the internal right and the external will take care of itself.

As for the pursuit of wisdom, here is what wisdom says to all: 'I love those who love me, and those who seek me find me' (Prov. 8:17). Whereas winning the gold medal is only for the best and the greatest, wisdom – the prize – is guaranteed to those who love it and pursue it.

But wisdom may cost you. Oh yes, it's free; it cannot be bought with money. It comes freely from God, but he can give it or withhold it. It comes with a price – the price being strict training and self-denial. As self-discipline, or strict training, is required to win an Olympic gold medal, so a different level of discipline prepares one for the greatest prize of all – wisdom. Insight. It is winning the gold medal of life.

Strict training

Whereas strict training in the Olympics is almost entirely physical – developing strong muscles, perfect co-ordination and effortless endurance – the strict training required for wisdom is spiritual: developing a Christ-centred mind, a heart after God, and a strong will to overcome temptation. It means resisting evil, swallowing your pride, accepting adversity with dignity, praying for your enemies, being unashamed of the gospel, being willing to kiss a good reputation goodbye. Jesus said, 'Whoever wants to be my disciple must deny themselves and take up their cross and follow me. For whoever wants to save their life will lose it, but whoever loses their life for me and for the gospel will save it' (Mark 8:34–35). Indeed, 'anyone who loves their life will lose it, while anyone who hates their life in this world will keep it for eternal life' (John 12:25).

In a word: self-discipline and the prize go together. The fear of the Lord inevitably brings you face to face with personal responsibility. Winston Churchill said that the price of greatness is responsibility. The question therefore is: *how much do you want wisdom?*

The NIV translation of Proverbs 4:7 doesn't specifically

say that wisdom costs. It says '*though* [my italics] it cost all you have' – which implies that it *could* cost you all you have. The point is, *if* it costs you all you have, it is still worth it.

And yet why should it cost? Why wouldn't God simply give it to you by your asking? Is it free or not? What exactly might be the 'cost' of wisdom? Whatever does Proverbs 4:7 mean by the words 'though it cost all you have' (NIV)?

The answer is, as we have seen, wisdom – which leads to the prize – is connected to the fear of the Lord. The *beginning* of wisdom is the fear of the Lord. And the Lord whom we revere and stand in awe of is a holy and jealous God. God wants to know how much are we willing to pay in order to win the prize? By 'cost' he does not mean reaching deep into your pocket for money. He means honouring a holy God by a holy lifestyle. Wisdom and an unholy lifestyle don't go together. A jealous God won't have this. And if you happen to be deeply involved in things that displease the Lord, yes, wisdom will cost you. The cost is giving up what has been so much a part of your life in order to get the prize. If strict training – self-discipline – is a requirement for the gold medal in the Olympics, so too is self-discipline needed to win the prize – which is more precious than gold.

First of all, this means that one must be *willing* to do whatever it takes – even if it means losing everything – in order to get the prize. I suspect that it affects three of the major things in life that most of us have to reckon with

– money, sex and power. This order is suggested by John when he told us not to love the world or the things in it, such as: 'the lust of the flesh, the lust of the eyes, and the pride of life' (1 John 2:15–16).

Money

Despite the heading, money itself is not the problem but *greed*. This is what John meant by the 'cravings' of sinful man and why he listed it first. 'Whoever loves money never has enough; whoever loves wealth is never satisfied with their income' (Eccles. 5:10). It is not money but the 'love of money' that is the root of all evil (1 Tim. 6:10). The love of money militates against wisdom. When making money becomes a priority, our judgment can be compromised and may even become warped so that we cannot think straight. It is often rooted in our not being satisfied with our needs being supplied; we want more.

It is our essential needs that God promises to supply (Phil. 4:19). This basically means food, shelter and clothing. In the Sermon on the Mount Jesus addressed the matter of how our heavenly Father accepts the responsibility for looking after us. He feeds the sparrow and clothes the lilies of the field. But we are more valuable than these, says Jesus. As God is responsible for looking after us, so we are responsible for seeking the kingdom of God first. The promise is that if we make the kingdom of God our priority, we will have all we need (Matt. 6:25–33).

Seeking first the kingdom of God is to choose the fear of the Lord. In other words, it is wisdom to seek the kingdom of God and not give in to excessive fear or greed. The moment though that greed slips in, we risk losing wisdom. When you lose wisdom, you lose the prize. This is why Jesus said it is very hard for a rich man to enter the kingdom of God (Matt. 19:23).

There are few people who can be trusted with wealth, and it is an exceedingly rare person who can maintain transparent integrity and make a lot of money at the same time. There are some, yes – but not many. The issue is: which do we prefer? More money or more wisdom?

The chance to earn money is the easiest thing in the world to justify, and it may be perfectly right to do so. God may lead you in that direction. But there is a caution: don't be swift to assume you are one of those who can gain the prize and earn a lot of money. I have watched how good people let financial opportunity come in – and lose integrity. The heart is deceitful above all things and incurably wicked; who can know it? (Jer. 17:9).

God has not promised to make you rich. He has promised to supply your need. That said, if you had the choice (and you do) between money and wisdom, which would you choose?

Are there boundaries that will help ensure you have not crossed over a line and thereby forfeited wisdom? I believe there are.

First, there is accountability. Are you accountable to trusted people who will tell you when you might be compromising your integrity? We all need people around us who will tell us the truth. Do you gather people around you who always tell you what you want to hear – or what you *need* to hear? If you say, 'It is nobody's business', I would lovingly warn you that this is a huge mistake. How much do you want the prize? If you are compromising your walk with God by the way you dismiss advice from good people concerning how you earn and handle money, would you not want to know it? In a multitude of counsellors there is safety (Prov. 15:22, AV). If you say, 'I am accountable only to God', I would reply: those are the famous last words of yesterday's man. Nobody is that spiritual that he or she does not need to be accountable to others. We all need all the input we can get if we are going for the prize.

However, I'm afraid it is highly possible to convince your 'accountability group' that you are being wholly transparent with them, and still be privately operating in a dangerous way. But it is up to *you* whether you want to be truly accountable to those who love you. Don't be a fool. Be accountable. Make sure you are not hiding secrets from them.

Second, are you gracious to the needy, the poor and the work of the Lord? Are you generous in your giving? Are you a tither? Tithing (one tenth of your income) to God is the minimum you should give to the Lord. Some can give more, but no one should ever give less. I have written a book on this subject – *The Gift of Giving* – in which I make the biblical case for tithing to your church. Also, are you sensitive to the needs of the poor? 'Whoever is kind to the needy honours God' (Prov. 14:31). 'Whoever is kind to the poor lends to the LORD, and he will reward them for what they have done' (Prov. 19:17).

Third, is your walk with Jesus Christ such that you can sense it when you grieve the Holy Spirit? I would encourage you to have the kind of relationship with the Lord that means you can *feel* it when you make a decision that is motivated by greed. You should *feel* it when you become 'in the flesh'. This kind of relationship with God is not just for high-profile Christians or those in full-time Christian work. It is for *everyone*. When you have your eye on the prize, you will be able to sense it when you cross a line that shows your motive is not honouring to God. 'So whether you eat or drink, or whatever you do, do it all for the glory of God' (1 Cor. 10:31).

There is one thing you can be sure of – and stake your life upon it: you will maintain personal integrity if you do everything for God's glory. There is no way you can live for the glory of God and be dishonest, untrue to yourself, or lack integrity.

This means being squeaky clean with money. It means paying your debts, and being totally honest in all your financial dealings – whether that be declaring your income for tax purposes or in business transactions. The fear of God must be the overriding factor in all your decisions concerning money.

There are two further principles that may apply here: (1) The Golden Rule: 'Do to others as you would have them do to you' (Luke 6:31). When it comes to money, if you treat another person as you would want to be treated, you will be maintaining integrity and will be a blessing to them. (2) Make every financial decision as if the whole world were watching. One day they might see your every decision! We will stand before God and give an account of everything we have done when on planet earth (2 Cor. 5:10). What if God chooses to unveil *all* our financial dealings before everyone? How would that make you feel? Live in the here and now in such a manner that you cannot possibly be embarrassed at the Judgment.

Sex

John speaks of the 'lust of the eyes' (1 John 2:16). Jesus said that one commits adultery in his heart if he looks at a woman 'lustfully'. Some scholars such as Michael Eaton and D. M. Carson think this could be understood as 'causing one to lust' (Matt. 5:28). This means you commit adultery if you intentionally cause another person to lust after you. For example, if a man uses seductive language – or touches a woman with the purpose of causing her to lust – he has committed adultery in his heart. If a woman dresses provocatively – or touches a man with the purpose of causing him to lust after her – she has committed adultery in her heart.

One of the most conspicuous themes in the book of Proverbs is the almost in-your-face warnings against dultery – and the immoral woman. 'For the lips of the adulterous woman drip honey, and her speech is smoother than oil; but in the end she is bitter as gall' (Prov. 5:3–4).

Wisdom will save one from the adulterous and 'from the wayward wife with her seductive words'. The message of Proverbs is clear: sexual immorality is not only unwise, but guarantees losing wisdom. When people lose their heads for sex outside marriage they therefore abandon hope in attaining to godly wisdom.

The biblical view of marriage is that it is heterosexual, monogamous and permanent. 'Marriage should be honoured by all and the marriage bed kept pure, for God will judge the adulterer and all the sexually immoral' (Heb. 13:4). Part of this judgment would be a gross lack of wisdom. Sex is to be confined to marriage alone. 'Drink water from your own cistern . . . may you rejoice in the wife of your youth . . . may her breasts satisfy you always, may you ever be intoxicated with her love. Why, my son, be intoxicated with another man's wife?' (Prov. 5:15, 18–20). Wisdom will keep you from 'the smooth talk of a wayward woman . . . a prostitute can be had for a loaf of bread, but another man's wife preys on your very life. Can a man walk on hot coals without his feet being scorched? So is he who sleeps with another man's wife; no one who touches her will go unpunished' (Prov. 6:24–29). 'But a man who commits adultery has no sense; whosoever does so destroys himself' (Prov. 6:32).

Sooner or later we all come face to face with sexual temptation. This is the way God made us. But giving in to it risks losing both an internal and external inheritance. Joseph could not have known that his external inheritance included being prime minister of Egypt. Had he committed adultery with Potipher's wife, he almost certainly would have forfeited an utterly brilliant career. He resisted sexual temptation (Gen. 39:10), later showed extraordinary wisdom with Pharaoh (Gen. 41:28–40), and became the link in preserving the children of Israel (Gen. 45:5–8).

I wrote a book several years ago *Is God for the Homosexual?* (Answer: yes). The universal response from the gay community was (1) they were surprised how compassionate I was toward gay people; and (2) what a pity I did not allow for gay people to indulge in sexual activity. Being gay is nothing new. That it is condemned in Scripture shows it existed in antiquity or there would be no need to refer to it. And yet all the references in Proverbs (that I can see) refer to heterosexual promiscuity. For that reason I would have preferred to leave the gay issue out of this book. But I cannot. Gay sex is not only on the rise but is now being zealously promoted by nearly everybody – not only by gays but heterosexuals. The growing consensus is that gay people are *entitled* to have sex since the overwhelming feeling nowadays is that this is the way they are made. But we do no favours to say, 'You are entitled to enjoy what your body craves'. That line is being repeated with more and more intensity. Even from within the church. Self-denial seems to have perished from the earth.

Regardless of sexuality, if it is the prize you want, then avoiding sexual sin is required.

Power

John calls it 'the pride of life' (1 John 2:16). In the present context, power is a word that touches our need for significance. It is traced to our ego, pride and self-esteem. It relates to the need to be admired. Some people are wired in such a manner that power is the only thing that gives them a feeling of significance. It is the desire for power – or the aspiration to be *seen* as having power – that has its origin in our egos. Whereas the need for sex stems from a physical desire, the desire for power is largely rooted in a wish – consciously or unconsciously – to make others envious. '. . . all toil and all achievement spring from one person's envy of another' (Eccles. 4:4). And yet sex and power are often closely connected. Some men aspire to power partly to impress women, and some women are attracted to men who have power – therefore a sexual ingredient is often in the mix when it comes to self-esteem.

When asked why he wanted to be president, John F. Kennedy replied, 'That's where the power is.' This is partly because of the need to control, partly to have influence, but also to be seen as a powerful leader. Such leadership may be in politics, in business, in law, in medicine or in the Church. Strong leaders, though, normally do not have high levels of humility. They are not so teachable, because they often think they know it all. This is why Solomon's request for wisdom was so pleasing to God.

Overcoming temptation: two kinds of genuine conversion

For reasons I cannot explain, there seem to be two types of conversions to Jesus Christ: spectacular and unspectacular. The former are more rare than the latter. In other words, most people who are genuinely converted to Christ continue to struggle with the same temptations they had before they were saved. Take drug addiction. I know a lady – Iris – who was a drug addict and prostitute in Texas. I have met her and invited her to speak at Westminster Chapel. Her story in a word: she read a Christian tract and gave her heart to the Lord – and was spectacularly converted: the desire for drugs completely left her. From the moment she prayed the prayer to receive Christ she lost *all* desire for heroin and also gave up prostitution. She began to devote herself to a ministry to drug addicts, and has led hundreds to the Lord. But she said candidly to me, 'Very, very few of them lose the craving for heroin. Few get saved like I did. I don't know why. They fight it with all their might and it is a tough battle.' I said, 'Do you think that those who struggle are as "saved" as those who have a dramatic instantaneous deliverance?' Her reply: 'Absolutely. Those who struggle are as converted by the Lord as those who have a miraculous deliverance. Those who struggle need more compassion, more attention, more follow-up and more prayer. They all know they must fight it because it is wrong.'

I know of a gay man – Dennis, a hymn writer whose songs are sung all over the world. He was led to the Lord by my close friend Jack Taylor. Dennis left his gay lifestyle and got married – and now has five children. But Dennis is rare – very rare – and this is a fact that must be faced. One should not expect gay people always to be instantly delivered – and changed into heterosexuals. Their proclivity may remain as it was. The issue is: should the gay person *fight* it like a person fights heroin? Or, since many homosexuals feel God 'made' them like this, are they not entitled to give in to their sexual proclivity?

I also know heterosexuals who have very strong libidos – and are genuinely converted. Some of them are amazingly delivered – and live a celibate lifestyle until they get married. Others never marry and still have to fight their sexual urges with all their being.

The point is, those who have a sudden deliverance from their past habits are not necessarily 'more converted', 'more saved' or 'more born again' than those who struggle.

Go for the gold

The heart of the matter is this: how much does winning the 'prize' mean? You can either cherish wisdom – and value coming into your inheritance more than anything else – or feel sorry for yourself and cave in to the pressure. Self-pity and a feeling of entitlement are twin temptations that *every* Christian must come to grips with.

I write these lines with strong feeling. I want the reader to know that I am totally sympathetic with the struggles many people face, living in a world of extreme loneliness, fierce temptation and (sometimes) without feeling a lot of grace from God. I would only say to you – with all the love and persuasiveness in my soul – *don't give up*. Accept your plight as similar to the 'strict training' that the Olympic athlete goes through to win the prize. The recipient hearing their national anthem when the gold medal is placed around their neck must be the greatest feeling on earth. Indescribable. But there is something better – and that is when Jesus looks at you and says 'Well done'.

Go for the gold.

Eve

It is interesting that the first time wisdom is implied in Holy Scripture was in the Garden of Eden when Eve believed that eating the forbidden fruit would make a person 'wise' (Gen. 3:6). So I raise the question: if seeking wisdom pleases God, why was Eve not commended for her quest for wisdom in partaking of the fruit? Answer: the idea of 'wisdom' that was offered in the Garden of Eden was not put there by God, but by Satan. Remember: *godly wisdom never counters what God has already said*. He commanded that one should not eat of the tree of the knowledge of good and evil (Gen. 2:17), but Satan said, 'God knows that when you eat of it your eyes will be opened, and you will be like God, knowing good and evil' (Gen. 3:5, ESV). Eve was deceived (2 Cor. 11:3; 1 Tim. 2:14). Any wisdom that is promised, but which is in fact rooted in disobedience to God's word, will always be counterfeit wisdom. Satan masquerades as an 'angel of light' (2 Cor. 11:14). What Satan succeeded in doing with Eve was to lure her away from God's command not to eat of the tree of the knowledge of good and evil. The rest, as they say, is history.

How much do you esteem wisdom?

I once pleaded with a well-known preacher to take some of my advice concerning a particular matter. I was convinced – as were many others – that he needed a word that would help him. I got nowhere with him, and gave up when he said to me, 'Why should I listen to you, R.T. – you only preach to hundreds and I have my thousands.' To repeat the earlier quip, 'You can always tell a successful man but you can't tell him much'!

Sometimes God withholds success from us in order to keep us teachable. I am quite sure I would never have invited certain people to preach for me at Westminster Chapel if we were already filled from top to bottom. I never forgot what Dr Martyn Lloyd-Jones used to say to me: 'The worst thing that can happen to a man is to succeed before he is ready.' When a person comes into power and prominence too soon it is often disastrous. People aim for the top – then achieve it. They are clever but, so often, not wise. Pride goes before destruction and a haughty spirit before a fall (Prov.

16:18). For some, sex is a person's downfall; for some others, it is one's pride.

How much do you esteem wisdom? If it is wisdom we want, we may be required to forfeit the praise and approval of people. The reason the Jews missed their Messiah came down to their choosing the fear of man rather than the honour that comes only from God (John 5:44). The wisdom of knowing the next step forward – receiving the honour from God – reaps far more benefits than the ego trip that the applause of people may provide.

If you had the choice whether to pray for your enemy (and know the prayer would be answered) or assume you have sufficient cleverness to press on without having to do such a thing, which would you choose? It may be that God will bring you to your knees – when you see your bankruptcy regarding a level of wisdom, to persuade you to pray for those who have wanted to destroy you. But if you got wisdom in the exchange, wouldn't that be worth it? 'What good is it for someone to gain the whole world, yet forfeit their soul?' (Mark 8:36).

You may ask: what is the connection between wisdom and sincerely praying for your enemy? I answer: Jesus said that our reward would be 'great' (Luke 6:27–35). There is no greater reward than wisdom. Moreover, what chiefly grieves the Holy Spirit in our minds is bitterness and unforgiveness (Eph. 4:30–32). I forfeit the presence of the mind of the Spirit – my definition of wisdom – when I give in to bitterness and refuse to forgive totally those who have sought to hurt me. But when we sincerely pray for our enemies, there will emerge in us a *level of clear thinking* that can be achieved in no other way.

Consider the amazing performance of Stephen, one of the Church's first deacons and the first martyr of the Christian Church, when he was called to answer to the Sanhedrin. His opponents were not able to withstand the wisdom and Spirit with which he spoke (Acts 6:10). What was Stephen's secret? The answer is found in his last words – just before he was stoned to death: 'Lord, do not hold this sin against them' (Acts 7:60). What a way to die!

The cost of the prize, then, is choosing the fear of the Lord. It includes delaying gratification of certain temptations – as in financial achievement, sexual gratification and gaining the praise of people. God may indeed want to bless you financially. He may bring the right person into your life to give you the companionship that Adam craved even before sin came into the world (Gen. 2:18). God may be pleased to exalt you and give you honour that you never dreamed possible.

But choosing the fear of the Lord means putting *his Word and his ways* first. The result will be the most wonderful, desirable, coveted and precious gift on this planet: *wisdom*. And a reward at the judgment seat of Christ.

Paul called it the prize. He wanted it more than anything. Do you?

6

The Gift of Wisdom

For to one is given through the Spirit the
utterance of wisdom. (1 Cor. 12:8, ESV)

Every good and perfect gift is from above, coming
down from the Father of the heavenly lights, who
does not change like shifting shadows. (Jas. 1:17)

One of the rather funny ironies pertaining to the discussion of wisdom and common grace (as seen in Chapter 2) is that unusual wisdom may come to a non-Christian – as in the case of Winston Churchill – and yet a genuine Spirit-filled Christian may be (so it might seem) utterly devoid of wisdom! It isn't funny, I know. But I have watched this over the years (you don't know whether to laugh or cry); some of God's dearest and most precious saints seem unable to show common sense.

And yet Paul did say quite candidly to the believers in Corinth: '. . . think of what you were when you were called. *Not many you were wise* by human standards; not many were influential; not many were of noble birth' (1

Cor. 1:26 – my italics). You might say: 'But this only refers to the way they were before they were saved.' Yes, and this suggests that most of them did not have the highest level of education or even intelligence. Remember that in the ancient Hellenistic world there was an assumption that philosophers – or those who could think philosophically – were the most valued. Certainly they were the most respected. It was the time and place in which the Platos and the Aristotles of this world were the supreme role models. And so, yes, this was their pre-conversion state. But whereas 1 Corinthians 1:26 depicts Christians before they were converted, there is no indication that the gift of wisdom is part of the package when a person is saved. Paul will even say that Christ is our wisdom: 'And because of him you are in Christ Jesus, who became to us wisdom from God, righteousness and sanctification and redemption' (1 Cor. 1:30, ESV). This means that Christ's wisdom, righteousness, sanctification and redemption are all imputed to us – that is, put to our credit – when we are saved. This way, God gets all the glory.

That said, *any* believer shows the highest level of wisdom when they discern and embrace the best offer one can get on this planet – namely, to know you will go to heaven when you die. Accepting the gift of eternal life vis-à-vis earthly fame and fortune is wisdom – commonsense discernment – if you ask me. Eternity lasts a long time. Better to go to heaven and be deprived of the good things of the here and now than go to hell a rich, famous or brilliant person.

Making a choice for eternal life therefore shows true wisdom. Those who are supposedly brilliant, but reject the offer of eternal life, show they are foolish and not wise.

Paul is saying that we should not be surprised that most Christians may not be the movers and shakers of this world. For some reason Christians are people who were chosen from a fallen human race, but who were not necessarily the brightest and most brilliant of men and women. God *could* have chosen the geniuses of this world, but he deliberately chose not to. Why? 'In the wisdom of God' the world through its wisdom did not know him, so God was pleased through 'the foolishness of what was preached to save those who believe' (1 Cor. 1:21). Indeed, those who are wise by human standards generally think that becoming a Christian is 'beneath' them. Paul said we preach Christ crucified – a stumbling block to Jews and 'foolishness to Gentiles' (1 Cor. 1:23).

Gifts in relation to the fruits of the Spirit

You may want to say: 'But surely if one is *full* of the Holy Spirit he or she would have the most wisdom?' No. This is why the qualifications for the earliest deacons were that they be 'full of the Spirit *and* wisdom' (Acts 6:3 – my italics). Not all Christians are endowed with great wisdom, although those given responsible positions are the ones who most need it. If being a Christian – or being filled with the Spirit – automatically included wisdom there would be no need to add that wisdom was also needed to be a deacon. Whereas wisdom is listed as a *gift* of the Holy Spirit in 1 Corinthians 12:8–10, wisdom is *not* listed as a *fruit* of the Spirit in Galatians 5:22–23: 'love, joy, peace, forbearance, kindness, goodness, faithfulness, gentleness and self-control'. However, the bestowal of '*gifts*' – whether these be wisdom, prophecy, miracles or speaking in tongues – is the sovereign work of the Spirit. For all *gifts* 'are empowered by one and the same Spirit, who apportions to each one individually *as he wills*' (1 Cor. 12:11, ESV – my italics). You and I therefore are not given a mandate to possess one of the gifts of the Spirit, but we are commanded to show all of the fruits of the Spirit. But note: we do have a mandate to *covet* or 'earnestly desire' the best gifts (1 Cor. 12:31).

We observed earlier that the wisdom that comes from 'above' in James 3:17 borders on some of the descriptions of *agape* love in 1 Corinthians 13. And yet wisdom and love are not the same, as we shall see below.

So where does wisdom as a *gift* come from? If a Christian has the gift of wisdom is it solely by the sovereign impartation of the Holy Spirit sometime after his or her conversion, or did he/she have wisdom by virtue of common grace before being saved? I answer: in some cases it was before that person was saved. Everyone needs to ask God for wisdom, but some seem to be endowed with this as a result of their genes. They were gifted in the first place. And yet not even the brightest and most intellectual of people who are converted are necessarily endowed with the gift of wisdom. They can be clever, but not wise. As we saw in Chapter 2, a London taxi driver may have more common sense than a university professor. In any case, it is my view that those in the Church who have the gift of wisdom probably have it naturally – before they were saved. Of course, this does not mean God cannot endow anyone with wisdom after he or she has been born again. Of course he can – James encouraged *everyone* to ask God for wisdom (Jas. 1:5)! It must mean therefore that any of us may ask for and receive wisdom – if only for the moment when it is needed. But it does not follow that all have the *gift* of wisdom.

Wisdom and leadership

All leaders need a maximum dose of wisdom. Indeed, all those who are given a high level of responsibility need a lot of wisdom. But not all have it, even in the Church. Some churches are like sheep without a shepherd, and sometimes – sadly – the shepherd is more like the sheep than a leader. This person wets his finger, holds it up in the air to see which way the wind is blowing, then moves in that direction – merely following the majority but calling it 'leadership'. Whether in politics or in the Church, some people strangely manage to reach a position of strategic authority yet be devoid of wisdom. You wonder how they got there, and it is very painful to observe it. I will never forget watching President Bill Clinton defend himself on television when the

Monica Lewinsky scandal had reached its height. My heart ached as he demonstrated an outrageous lack of wisdom. He was one of the greatest politicians in US history, and so brilliant in many ways, but showed utter folly in his undisciplined personal life and his unwise defensiveness afterwards.

It can also be painful for leaders having to lead people who so lack wisdom. But that is why leaders are leaders; they lead sheep who are naturally prone to go astray, who have a 'herd' instinct, and think the grass is greener on the other side of the fence. This requires a leader to have wisdom and a high dose of patience – and also *agape* love. To the person who has wisdom, things are clear – namely, he or she knows what to do next. But when you are dealing with people who can't see the right thing to do next – even when it is pointed out to them – it can be exasperating. The gift of wisdom therefore needs to be baptised in *agape* love – or the leadership will be counterproductive.

The perfect combination for leadership is wisdom and love. But some people have wisdom without love, and don't suffer fools gladly; while others have love but not wisdom – and do stupid things.

I invited Arthur Blessitt, the man who has carried the cross around the world (to whom I shall refer again in Chapter 8), to preach at Westminster Chapel for six weeks in April and May 1982. He initiated things that had never been done before: calling people forward to make a public decision, singing choruses as well as the old hymns, and witnessing in the streets – which resulted in the Pilot Light ministry. I'm ashamed to admit I did not have the courage to initiate these things. So after he went on to his next place to minister, I had a hard decision to make: whether to go back to 'business as usual' (which would have pleased some of my church members) or to keep up what Arthur had started. I had to face the issue as to whether what Arthur had started was truly of God – either God had brought him to us, or he hadn't. But I knew in my heart that God had sent him, so I decided to keep up what he had started. It was the most pivotal – and the best – decision I made in twenty-five years in London. But it also got me into more trouble than anything I had done up to that time. Some people who had been my best supporters were suddenly unhappy. Even many of those who supported me in the changes were nervous. In fact, we possibly got more support from people outside the Chapel than from within it.

Satan seizes any opportunity to cause division, and this is one of the reasons that the gift of wisdom is needed. Wisdom is at the top of the list when Paul began identifying the various gifts of the Spirit, but, sadly, it is the last gift that some people seem to covet.

Is the gift of wisdom permanent?

One of the first questions people ask is whether the gift of wisdom resides permanently in a person or whether it emerges in and out as needed. The wisdom we are encouraged to pray for in James 1:5 is probably not the gift of wisdom as in 1 Corinthians 12:8, but the needed presence of the mind of the Holy Spirit in a crisis. Generally speaking, the gift of wisdom is a permanent one, and Paul's use of the word 'gift' in 1 Corinthians 7 suggests this. Paul claimed that he himself had a particular gift – namely, to live without the need for sexual fulfilment. He accepted the fact that most people need to get married, and then said: 'I wish that all men were as I am', implying he had a gift that enabled him to live without a wife. Some think Paul was a widower; some think he was able to travel long periods without his wife. Whatever the reason, most men do not have this gift. 'But each of you has your own gift from God,' Paul continued; 'one has this gift, another has that' (1 Cor. 7:7). These lines suggest the use of the word 'gift' to be a permanent possession – or at least one that is present for a while. This is partly why I think Paul meant that the gifts of the Spirit tend to reside permanently in a person.

However, it does not follow that the gifts of the Spirit in a person are infallible. Any gift will be in 'measure' (Rom. 12:3). All faith has its limits – except Jesus' faith; he alone had the Spirit without limit (John 3:34). All fruits have their limit, for if a person is never at fault in what he says he is a perfect man (Jas. 3:2). No one is perfect; if we claim to be without sin we are deceived and the truth is not in us (1 John 1:8).

All gifts therefore have their limit. For example, the person with the gift of wisdom does not always demonstrate perfect wisdom. The person with the gift of healing does not see every single person that they pray for healed. A prophecy from a prophetically gifted person who often gets it right may not always be totally accurate, as in the case of Agabus. In his prediction of a famine, Agabus got it right (Acts 11:28), but he got it wrong in the details of Paul being turned over to the Gentiles (compare Acts 21:10–11 with what actually happened in Acts 23–26). Although what Agabus prophesied concerning Paul was generally true, he missed it in the details.

At the natural level, no intelligence or human wisdom reaches the zenith of infallibility. Whether it be the US Central Intelligence Agency or MI6 in the UK, perfection is not attainable. These two organisations almost certainly have some of the greatest minds in the West – but intelligence does not always mean wisdom. All the intelligence agencies can do is to estimate a situation to the best of their ability – horrible mistakes are still made.

Ahithophel

Ahithophel had been King David's most trusted adviser: 'Now in those days the advice that Ahithophel gave was like that of one who enquires of God. That was how both David and Absalom regarded all of Ahithophel's advice' (2 Sam. 16:23). Athithophel had the gift of wisdom, but he was not loyal to David. It is a grim reminder that wisdom and loyalty do not always reside in the same person. Here is what happened. Absalom, David's son, stole the hearts of the people and forced King David into exile. Athithophel sided with Absalom. It was utterly shocking and painful to have one's own son betray him, but David did not remotely dream he would lose Ahithophel too.

Ahithophel's betrayal therefore goes to show that a person having extraordinary wisdom does not presuppose that person's loyalty. I have concluded over the years that the one thing you can never know for sure about a person you meet – or someone you interview – is whether he or she will be loyal. There is no test on earth that can be done to guarantee the person you employ or confide in will be loyal. If you employ someone, give that person a position, confide in him or her, or trust that person to be committed to you, I can only say that if he or she turns out to be loyal you are most fortunate indeed. This would be true with a spiritual leader, a banker, an administrative assistant, a secretary, a person in whom you invest great responsibility, a minister, a vicar, a solicitor or barrister, a doctor or teacher. If that person is loyal, you are blessed.

King David was devastated when he heard that 'Ahithophel is among the conspirators with Absalom' (2 Sam. 15:31). David wept; it was the lowest point in his life. All he could do was to pray, and he did just that: 'O Lord, turn Ahithophel's counsel into foolishness'. I don't know how much faith David had that his prayer would be answered, but it was. Absalom asked Ahithophel for advice as to what to do in order to defeat David completely, and Ahithophel told Absalom exactly what to do to secure his kingship and to defeat David for ever. Had Absalom followed Ahithophel, he would have remained king; his advice would have undoubtedly worked. But Absalom also asked Hushai – who was secretly loyal to David – for his advice. Lo and behold, Absalom listened to Hushai – and the result was that Absalom was defeated and David was able to return to Jerusalem and his kingship was restored. In the meantime Ahithophel could see what was happening and committed suicide (2 Sam. 16:21–17:23). This further shows that a person with the gift of wisdom is indeed fallible.

The gift of wisdom enables a person to see from A to Z in a given situation. However, seeing from A to B is at least a *bit* of wisdom – after all, it means you know the next step forward. But the true gift of wisdom is having the ability to see from the beginning to the end in one stroke. It is the ability to discern a situation thoroughly – the implications, what will be regretted and what will be valued, after that situation is over. This is an exceedingly rare gift.

The difference between wisdom and love

Wisdom and love both come from God. However, as we have seen, the wisdom that comes from 'above' in James 3 sounds an awful lot like the love described in 1 Corinthians 13 which is patient, kind, not arrogant or irritable (1 Cor. 13:4–5). Likewise, the wisdom James describes is not abrasive or judgmental and is full of mercy (Jas. 3:17). To put it another way, the wisdom James outlines seems more like a fruit of the Spirit, as in Galatians 5, than the gift of wisdom as in 1 Corinthians 12:10. The fruit of the Spirit is 'love, joy, peace, forbearance, kindness, goodness, faithfulness, gentleness and self-control' (Gal. 5:22–23). I think this is why the gift of wisdom is not put forward as a 'fruit' of the Spirit. Indeed, the gift of wisdom *could* lack the fruit of the Spirit – as in love, patience, kindness and gentleness. Wisdom without the fruit of the Spirit can be acerbic and short on kindness.

This further helps us to realise that having true wisdom does not make one infallible. The person who has the gift of wisdom needs a lot more than mere wisdom if he or she is going to be a great blessing to people. What a pity if wisdom is displayed – showing clearly what needs to be done, what is right, and what will happen if you do it – but is not accepted by others because the wrong spirit accompanied the gift. I have seen this happen. A person can be right, yet still be wrong when a wise action is not immersed in love.

For this reason, wisdom needs to be laced with humility. In the perfect world wisdom would automatically encompass patience. Indeed, 'a person's wisdom yields patience; it is to one's glory to overlook an offence' (Prov. 19:11). But there are levels of wisdom. The book of Proverbs possibly points to the highest levels of wisdom – which only Jesus demonstrated. If a man had perfect wisdom, he would never lose his temper or give in to pride. This is why Paul urges that a person should not be wise in their own eyes because the most prudent person can so easily take themselves too seriously (Rom. 12:16, ESV). In fact, *any* gift of the Spirit is vulnerable to pride – whether it is wisdom, prophecy or healing. 'What do you have that you did not receive? And if you did receive it, why did you boast as though you did not?' (1 Cor. 4:7). Some people with the gift of speaking in tongues have probably done damage to the reputation of the charismatic gifts because of their zeal to get others to speak in tongues. Some are more evangelistic about tongues than they are about the gospel. Some sincere Christians at times imply that one is more spiritual or godly *because* they speak in tongues. This is not true, and promoting this notion shows a lack of wisdom. All of the gifts of the Spirit should be matched by the fruits of the Spirit.

An old man aged about eighty used to come to Westminster Chapel on Sunday nights, having been at Speaker's Corner in Hyde Park for most of the afternoon. In our evening communion service for some reason he stood up and began speaking in tongues. That was just about barely OK with most of our congregation, as he was a sweet old soul. But then he gave the interpretation of his tongue, using King James Version language: 'Thus saith the Lord, I am with thee, I will bless thee, oh if thou wouldst call on my name . . .' When he did it the first time it seemed harmless, but he continued to do exactly the same thing at every Sunday evening communion service. I did not question his gift of tongues, but I was nervous whether he had much wisdom and a true gift of interpretation of tongues. The latter would be far more impressive if another person had stood up and spoken, but he never gave them a chance. Moreover, after a few weeks his speaking in tongues and interpretation became more of a performance. It did not edify, and there was an apparent absence of wisdom in what he did. He did not seem to notice that he was not blessing the people. I finally went over to him and spoke as gently as I could, but he was offended and never came back to us again.

There has been a tendency in some parts of the Church to stress the gifts of the Spirit more than the fruits – although in some places it is the other way around. What might be termed 'conservative evangelicals' have emphasised the fruits of the Spirit, while 'charismatics' tend to spend more time on the gifts of the Spirit. The reality is that *both* are needed. True wisdom, it seems to me, is to call for an emphasis on both gifts and fruits of the Spirit – equally.

7

Blind Spots

... you, then, who teach others, do you not teach
yourself? You who preach against stealing, do you
steal? You who say that people should not commit
adultery, do you commit adultery? (Rom. 2:19–22)

You say, 'I am rich; I have acquired wealth
and do not need a thing.' But you do not
realise that you are wretched, pitiful,
poor, blind and naked. (Rev. 3:17)

Wisdom has its limits. As every believer has faith in
'measure' (Rom. 12:3), so too with wisdom. Nobody
is perfect.

In this chapter we will see how wisdom will always be paralleled with a blind spot. A person may have incredible wisdom
about a situation, but not have much objectivity about himself.
A blind spot is enough to keep us humble – that is, if we will
admit to a blind spot! The truth is, we all have them.

A blind spot is something that keeps you from seeing
what is there. When it comes to our physical eyes it is called

scotoma, an obscuration of the visual field. When it comes to driving a car, a blind spot is the area around the vehicle that cannot be directly observed by the driver while at the controls. Sometimes one comes close to having an accident because there is a very small area that neither my car's rear-view mirror or wing mirror reflects – for example, seeing a car that has come alongside. So when driving I am always turning my neck to see directly rather than trust my mirrors. It can be scary.

But the scariest blind spot of all is with regard to my own perception of things – either of other people, of what I believe to be true, or my opinion of myself. A blind spot is something that stops me from seeing what is there. It is caused by my sin, my self-righteousness. A blind spot may keep me from seeing a particular truth in Scripture; the truth about another person; or from having transparent honesty concerning my own weaknesses. In other words, it stops me from seeing when I am in the wrong. I could even be so enamoured with someone that I see no fault in that person. 'Love is blind', as the saying goes. On other other hand, I could be so upset with someone that I am unable to see any good in that person. It is my blind spot. A blind spot may be the result of a bias or prejudice. Others can see this – but I cannot. It may be jealousy, which others can see – but I cannot. It may be pride. Others can see it, but I cannot.

Our blind spot keeps us from having true objectivity about ourselves. It is often the unwillingness to see ourselves in a way that is patently obvious to everybody else. The truth is too painful, so this blind spot renders us unteachable, unreachable, and sometimes causes us to live in denial. As the famous Scottish poem put it:

> O *wad some Power the giftie gie us*
> *To see oursels as ithers see us!*
>   Robert Burns, (1759–96)

Any measure of wisdom that is imparted to us comes with a blind spot. Even the highest level of wisdom is accompanied by a blind spot. But we actually *need* our blind spots.

The wisest, most godly and the most brilliant people have their blind spots. John Calvin said that in every saint there is something 'reprehensible'. Why? It is because the wiser we are the greater the temptation is to take ourselves too seriously. Great wisdom does not eradicate a huge ego. The awareness of a blind spot should keep us humble. It is not unlike Paul's 'thorn in the flesh'. Although Paul prayed three times for his thorn – whatever it was – to go away, he concluded that it was given to him to stop him from being conceited (2 Cor. 12:7). For the same reason Paul specifically cautioned that we must never be wise in our own eyes, and he also warned the Christians in Rome lest they be 'wise in your own sight' (Rom. 11:25, ESV). He even repeated it: 'Never be wise in your own sight' (Rom. 12:16, ESV).

The reason is this. It is so easy to feel good about ourselves when we think we have done something right – whether this is offering a good word of advice, or giving financially to the work of God. For example, we all know when we have given an amount of money to someone – whether to the Church or to a charity. We know the exact amount. We know whether we tithe, don't we? And yet Jesus said – in the context of giving – not to let our left hand know what our right hand is doing (Matt. 6:3). This means we should avoid *telling ourselves* what we have given. We know of course that we have given, and exactly what we have given, but Jesus meant that we should not think about it – to put it out of our minds.

It is this same principle that lurks around the issue of how one becomes a Christian. As long as you point to your own righteousness – and see it as the reason you are fit to go to heaven – you have no hope of being saved. It is when you see that your righteousness is as 'filthy rags' in God's sight (Isa. 64:6) and ask for mercy that you are a candidate to be saved. And yet even after conversion, one must still fight against self-righteousness. We never outgrow the need of mercy as believers; and mercy is always the first thing we should ask for when we pray (Heb. 4:16). The moment we point to our accomplishments, we negate effectiveness in prayer.

So with wisdom. I should not allow a feeling of glee or gloating to set in when I have demonstrated what I believe to be wisdom. When I think I have given a word that was spot on – whether in a sermon or to an individual – I should refuse to dwell on it. I must put it out of my mind – and not look back. The flesh will exult if given a chance; Satan will move in quickly to make us feel too good about ourselves – only to set us up to be conceited. This pride anticipates a downfall (Prov. 16:18).

Smugness

There is a notable absence of humility among some academics, who can be intolerant of mediocrity. But I'm afraid this is also true of the most 'holy' people. Many Christians who truly pursue godliness and self-discipline are often blind to the inevitable danger of smugness. Sadly we easily become all too aware of an aspiration for holiness, purity, and the feeling that comes from pleasing the Lord – and then become proud of it. When people become self-conscious of their godly attainments, lukewarmness rather than holy fire sets in. The result is a blatant blind spot: 'I need nothing', they say, when in fact they are 'blind', said Jesus (Rev. 3:17).

What are we to do? Answer: postpone any judgment of ourselves until we get God's final and infallible verdict – when he will 'bring to light what is hidden in darkness and will expose the motives of the heart. At that time each will receive their praise from God' (1 Cor. 4:5). In the meantime, said Paul, 'I do not even judge myself' (1 Cor. 4:3).

Mind you, this was not always the case, for Jesus changed the way we should look at ourselves. Read the Old Testament. Although it is the word of God as much as the

New Testament, I have to admit that I sometimes cringe when I read of some major figures in the Old Testament. Nehemiah unashamedly prayed, 'Remember me with favour, my God, for all I have done for these people' (Neh. 5:19). Hezekiah prayed, 'Remember, LORD, how I have walked before you faithfully and with wholehearted devotion and have done what is good in your eyes' (2 Kings 20:3). Even David said, 'I have been blameless before him and have kept myself from sin. The LORD has rewarded me according to my righteousness, according to the cleanness of my hands in his sight' (Ps. 18:23–24). I rather think David wrote this in his early days – before he fell into adultery with Bathsheba and then killed her husband Uriah (2 Sam. 11). When we remember this sort of legacy from many notable saints in the Old Testament – especially men like Nehemiah – we can see how the Pharisees kept up this way of thinking, and consequently resented Jesus. The Pharisees wanted everybody to see how righteous they were (Matt. 23:5). Jesus, on the other hand, urged that our giving, praying and fasting be done in secret in order that God alone would know what we do (Matt. 6:1–6, 16–18).

In this chapter I have selected a few Old Testament figures in order to show their blind spots so that we might see our own, and thus, as much as possible, avoid making the same mistakes.

Have you ever observed a person whom you thought should be so grateful – and then watched them show utter ingratitude? You ask, 'How could a person as intelligent and clever as that be so blind?' Have you observed a person whom you thought was as godly as they come do or say something that shocks you?

Thank God for them. A blind spot should help to keep us all humble – that is, if we have the honesty, integrity and objectivity about ourselves to see what others see.

Sarah and Abraham

Abraham sincerely believed God's promise that he would give him a son – that a male child would come from his own body (Gen. 15:4–6). But after a while no child had come. Sarah had a suggestion: that Abraham sleep with Hagar, her servant. This 'wisdom' would be debated for centuries. Abraham took Sarah's advice, and Ishmael was born. For the next thirteen years Abraham believed that Ishmael was the promised child that God intended. Although there would be a great purpose and plan for Ishmael, God told Abraham – quite unexpectedly – that Sarah, aged ninety, would conceive. Abraham laughed, as did Sarah. But then Isaac came along (Isaac means 'he laughs'). Isaac was in fact the promised child, but intense rivalry emerged between Ishmael and Isaac. So Sarah said to Abraham, 'Get rid of that slave woman and her son, for that slave woman's son will never share in the inheritance with my son Isaac.'

Sarah's first suggestion – that Abraham sleep with Hagar – was not (apparently) God's idea. But in the end it turned out that God had a purpose and plan in all this. However, Sarah's pivotal word this second time was different. God immediately 'owned' what she insisted upon – that Ishmael must go. God said to Abraham, 'Do not be so distressed about the boy [Ishmael] and your slave woman [Hagar]. Listen to whatever Sarah tells you, because it is through Isaac that your offspring will be reckoned. I will make the son of the slave into a nation also, because he is your offspring' (Gen. 21: 12–13). Sarah's first suggestion was questionable, although God promised that Ishmael would become a nation. But Sarah's second word – that Abraham cast out Ishmael – was the very wisdom of God. Painful though it was for Abraham, he realised that Sarah had got it right this time.

Jacob

Jacob was the father of twelve sons, and from them came the twelve tribes of Israel. I used the title of one of Shakespeare's plays for the title of my book on Jacob – *All's Well that Ends Well*. For Jacob was so full of blind spots that I could finish the rest of this present book with them! And yet this is so encouraging, for his life is perhaps the best example of my favourite verse – Romans 8:28: 'And we know that all things work together for good to them that love God, to them who are the called according to *his* purpose' (AV).

I will only call attention to two of Jacob's blind spots – his role as a father and a husband. He had no idea of the ill effect he was having on his sons when he showed such unashamed partiality to Joseph. Joseph was the son of his favourite wife – Rachel – and Jacob made Joseph a robe of many colours (Gen. 37:3). This understandably made the other sons jealous. Therefore Jacob's love for Joseph did Joseph no favours. It led to Jacob losing Joseph for most of their lives. His brothers sold Joseph to the Ishmaelites – their Plan B (they would have killed him had not the Ishmaelites shown up at the right moment) – never expecting to see Joseph again. One cannot excuse the brothers of Joseph for their wickedness, but there is no doubt that Jacob's failure as a parent was largely at the bottom of it all.

There is more: the way Jacob treated ten of his sons over the years. When the sons returned from Egypt, having been sent by Jacob to buy food in the time of famine, the sons told their father that the prime minister demanded to see all eleven sons – including Benjamin, the other son of his beloved Rachel. Jacob's horrible reaction was: 'My son will not go down there with you; his brother [Joseph] is dead and he [Benjamin] is the only one left' (Gen. 42:38). Ponder these words – first, 'my son'. Only Benjamin mattered to Jacob. In case one does not pick up on this, Jacob added: 'he is the only one left'. What? *All ten* were Jacob's sons – standing there in front of their father! But Jacob treated them as if they did not matter. What a hurtful thing for a father to say to his children.

Many church leaders have not been the best of parents, and I must put myself in this category. In my book *Totally Forgiving Ourselves* I speak candidly of how I put my church and sermon preparation first, thinking I was putting God first. I now believe had I put my family first, I would have preached just as well; but I can't get those twenty-five years in London back. It was a horrific blind spot in me that needed divine forgiveness.

Leah and Rachel

Jacob fell in love with Rachel, the beautiful daughter of Laban. But when Jacob thought he was marrying Rachel he was tricked by her father Laban and was forced to marry the older and less attractive Leah. Jacob eventually got Rachel too, but Leah – the unloved wife – had an advantage over Rachel: Leah bore Jacob children, while Rachel was barren. When Leah had a son she said, 'Surely my husband will love me now'. After her second son was born she said, 'Because the LORD heard that I am not loved, he gave me this one too.' After her third son (Levi), Leah said, 'Now at last my husband will become attached to me, because I have borne him three sons.' But sadly Jacob loved only Rachel. When the fourth son (Judah) was born to Leah, she demonstrated a most extraordinary spirit that could be the crowning wisdom for every unloved woman: 'This time I will praise the LORD' (Gen. 29:33–35).

Leah showed godly wisdom. Instead of pinning her hopes on Jacob finally loving her, she turned to the Lord and got her joy from him: 'I will praise the Lord'. Countless unloved women in human history have seen Leah as a role model. But there is an interesting ironic footnote: Leah's sons did more for the kingdom of God in the end, for Levi became the tribe that produced the Levitical priesthood. The Messiah – Jesus Christ – would come through the tribe of Judah.

Joseph

Joseph's blind spot was that he not only lacked objectivity about himself, but was unaware how he was perceived by his peers. One of the first things said about Joseph was that he brought bad reports about his brothers to their father. No one likes a tattle-tale. Then came the previously mentioned coat of many colours. The only thing worse than making it was wearing it – which Joseph did without any concern as to how this was perceived by these ten brothers.

But there is more; Joseph had an unusual prophetic gift. It concerned dreams. When he told his dreams to his brothers, they hated him all the more. The dreams clearly indicated that these ten brothers would bow down to Joseph one day. The dreams were of God – no doubt about that – but did Joseph have to tell them? But he did, and that was his mistake. I sometimes think God would show us more if we could keep quiet about it, but Joseph couldn't stop himself. 'I had another dream', he unwisely told his brothers: '. . . this time the sun and the moon and eleven stars were bowing down to me' (Gen. 37:9). You didn't need to be Sigmund Freud to interpret that dream. This is when the brothers decided to kill Joseph.

Wisdom should give us not only objectivity about ourselves; we should also realise how we are being perceived by those around us. Those who are impervious to this show a gross lack of wisdom. Nobody's perfect; we all are going to offend, no matter how hard we try not to. But Joseph's blind spot led him to such alienation of his own brothers that they wanted him completely out of the way. God used this turn of events, of course; he always does. But it is hardly wisdom when we don't make an effort to avoid unnecessary offence.

Deborah and Jael

Deborah was a prophetess, one of the judges in the book of Judges. She was leading Israel at the time when Jabin, a wicked king of Canaan, and his commander Sisera, had cruelly oppressed the Israelites for twenty years. The Israelites cried to the Lord for help. One day Deborah sent for Barak and prophesied to him: 'The LORD, the God of Israel, commands you: "Go, take with you ten thousand men of Naphtali and Zebulun and lead them up to Mount

Tabor. I will lead Sisera, the commander of Jabin's army, with his chariots and his troops to the River Kishon and give him into your hands"' (Judges 4:6–7).

But Barak was a weak man. He said to Deborah, 'If you go with me, I will go; but if you don't go with me, I won't go.' Deborah agreed to go, but she gave this prophetic caution – also showing wisdom and sensitivity with regard to the male ego: 'Because of the way you are doing this, the honour will not be yours, for the Lord will hand Sisera over to a woman.' That threat did not bother Barak, and the result was that Israel triumphed decisively over their enemy. It came when a shrewd and courageous woman named Jael killed the king Jabin (Judges 4).

So the glory did go to Jael (Judges 5:24), to say nothing of Deborah. But the ultimate irony is when Barak – a coward – is mentioned in the great faith chapter of the Bible, in Hebrews 11:32. But why Barak, and not Deborah or Jael? I think Barak's faith is commended (1) because he honestly admitted to his lack of faith without Deborah, and (2) because of his willingness to let women have the glory in this decisive battle in Israel's history.

Gideon

Gideon is listed as a man of faith in Hebrews 11:32. He was raised up in ancient Israel in their time of dire need. He led the Israelites to a major victory over the Midianites. So far, so good. He showed true greatness when he refused – at their request – to rule over them: 'I will not rule over you, nor will my son rule over you. The Lord will rule over you.' This shows amazing devotion to God – utterly eschewing the kind of leadership that lesser men would have grasped with both hands.

But that sadly is not the end of the story. Gideon had a blind spot. 'I do have one request,' he said to them, 'that each of you give me an earring from your share of the plunder.' Oh dear – I wish he had not said that, but he did. Surprise, surprise, they answered: 'We'll be glad to give them.' They did, and the weight of the gold rings came to seventeen hundred shekels and more. Gideon made the gold into an ephod (which was clothing, like a vestment worn by the high priest), which he placed in Ophrah, his town. 'All Israel prostituted themselves by worshipping it there, and it became a snare to Gideon and his family' (Judges 8:27).

Gideon should have seen this coming, but he didn't. It was a blind spot in a great man.

Jephthah

Hebrews 11 is known as the 'faith' chapter of the Bible. Certain people in this chapter are described because of the extraordinary things they achieved by persistent faith – like Enoch, Noah, Abraham, Isaac, Jacob, Joseph and Moses.

Jephthah earned a place in Hebrews 11:32 alongside Gideon, Barak, David and Samuel. He was 'a mighty warrior', but also had a strong intellect. He had a thorough recall and grasp of Israel's history. When the Ammonites accused Israel of stealing the land from them, Jephthah responded with a full account of the prehistory of this accusation. He showed that the Ammonites had no 'right' to the land (Judges 11:14–28). He made the case that God himself clearly and unmistakably had won the battles for Israel, and the Ammonites should concede this. But they would not. 'Then the Spirit of the Lord came upon Jephthah,' and he proceeded to fight the Ammonites.

So far, so good – but Jephthah's blind spot lay right at the point of his genius. Having made the case that it was the *Lord* who fought Israel's battles, Jephthah felt he had to coerce him and further endear himself to God by making a vow – as if this were needed to persuade God to step in! It was utterly unnecessary for him to do this. Israel's battles were always the Lord's. It was in his commentary regarding Jephthah in the book of Judges that John Calvin made the statement, 'In every saint there is something reprehensible.'

Jephthah made a vow that would eclipse all the good he had done up to that point. As Richard Nixon will be remembered for Watergate, so Jephthah will be remembered for his foolish vow. A vow in the Old Testament is the same thing as swearing an oath. You had to keep it if you made it. He vowed to God that if he would defeat the Ammonites, 'Whatever comes out of the door of my house to meet me when I return from the Ammonites will be the Lord's, and I will sacrifice it as a burnt offering' (Judges 11:31). It was so foolish and unnecessary.

Israel won the battle. But when Jephthah returned to his home, 'who should come out to meet him but his daughter, dancing to the sound of tambourines! She was an only child . . . [Jephthah exclaimed], "Oh no, my daughter! You have brought me down and I am devastated. I have made a vow to the LORD that I cannot break"' (Judges 11:34–35).

A blind spot can be costly.

Samson

There are three men – two of which are mentioned in Hebrews 11:32 (Samson and David) – who have in common a similar blind spot: a sexual weakness. The third is Solomon.

Samson's ultimate fall came when he succumbed to Delilah's charm and manipulation. He had refused to reveal to her the secret of his great strength. He must have known that she was not his loyal friend. But his libido blinded him to the obvious. When she accused him of not really loving her, he gave in and told her that his secret was his uncut hair. So she cut it off and Samson lost everything: the Philistines gouged out his eyes and bound him with bronze shackles. But when his hair grew back his strength returned and he got revenge, killing more of the enemy when he died than while he lived (Judges 16:30). His accomplishment in death won him a place as a man of faith in Hebrews 11, showing once again how all things work together for good to them that love God (which Samson did) and are called according to his purpose (which Samson was). But what a price to pay for the lack of sexual control!

David

David's affair with Bathsheba has already been mentioned. His blind spot consisted in thinking he was special – even above the word of God. He knew exactly what the Seventh Commandment says: You shall not commit adultery (Exod. 20:14). He also knew the penalty for adultery: death. He thought this should apply to everybody but himself. For David was now king. He knew how God had been with him over the years – from the defeat of Goliath to gaining the kingship. He wrote many psalms. He brought the Ark of the Covenant to Jerusalem. He was told by God that Messiah would come through him. He is the only person in the Bible called a man after God's own heart (1 Sam. 13:14; Acts 13:22). He was special – but God is no respecter of those who ignore his laws. Even a man after God's own heart cannot bend the rules and expect special treatment.

David committed adultery with Bathsheba, then tried to cover it up by having her husband Uriah killed. David thought he had got away with it, for it was probably two years before Nathan the prophet came to him and exposed his sin. So David – the man after God's own heart – got caught. More than that, he was punished. What followed in the ensuing years was drastic. Nathan told him that although David's sin was forgiven, the sword would not depart from his house (2 Sam. 12:10) – and it didn't. Absalom killed his brother Amnon for committing incest with their sister. After being in exile, Absalom returned to Jerusalem and stole the hearts of the people and David was in exile. But God in the end rescued David, and Absalom was killed and lost everything. David was restored to the kingship. But the price he paid added up to one thing: the adultery wasn't worth it.

David's blind spot resulted in perhaps the greatest personal sins of any figure in the Old Testament – adultery and murder. Just for an afternoon of sex . . .

Bathsheba

Bathsheba is notorious for her fatal affair with King David. But in the end, having married David, she proved invaluable to the future of Israel. The aged king apparently forgot he had promised that Solomon would be his successor. During a most critical time Adonijah, another son of David, decided he would be the next king. Even Joab, David's number one commander, sided with Adonijah, and so Adonijah was making headway in securing the kingship. Nathan the prophet cautioned Bathsheba that Adonijah, not Solomon, was within moments of becoming king. She immediately went to King David and reminded him of his oath to Solomon. At the very last minute Bathsheba showed acute wisdom when she persuaded David to step in. This came in the nick of time (1 Kings 1) and Solomon became king.

Solomon

Perhaps the greatest mystery of all is how Solomon – commonly alleged to be the wisest man who ever lived – could be so unwise? He was famous for his wisdom. His request for wisdom pleased God so much that he was given things he had not even requested – wealth, riches and honour 'such as no king who was before you ever had and none after you will have' (2 Chron. 1:12). The Queen of Sheba visited Solomon, and talked with him about 'all she had on her mind'. Moreover, he answered 'all her questions; nothing was too hard for him to explain to her' (2 Chron. 9:1–2). The books of Proverbs and Ecclesiastes are said to have been written by Solomon. His accomplishments were vast, far greater than any king before or after him.

But he did not finish well. His kingship ended under a cloud in his latter years. How could anybody with such wisdom and knowledge allow his extraordinary career to come to an end with sadness?

Solomon's first mistake was when he made an alliance with Pharaoh king of Egypt and married his daughter (1

Kings 3:1). But there is more. He loved 'many foreign women besides Pharaoh's daughter' – Moabites, Ammonites, Edomites, Sidonians and Hittites. These were from nations about which the Lord told his people the Israelites, 'You must not intermarry with them, because they will surely turn your hearts after their gods' (1 Kings 11:2). Despite this command, Solomon 'held fast to them in love'. He had 700 wives and 300 concubines, 'and his wives led him astray' (v. 3). As he grew old, Solomon's wives turned his heart after other gods and he was no longer devoted to the Lord as the heart of David his father had been. In a word: 'So Solomon did evil in the eyes of the LORD' (1 Kings 11:6). He built a high place for worship to other gods for one reason: 'for all his foreign wives, who burned incense and offered sacrifices to their gods'. God became angry with Solomon because his heart had turned away from him. He said to Solomon, 'Since this is your attitude and you have not kept my covenant . . . I will most certainly tear the kingdom away from you' (1 Kings 11:11). It was, and is, so sad.

Solomon's blind spot was sexual attraction to foreign women and marrying them. They led him astray and caused him to forfeit God's pleasure. Here is a man who had everything – incalculable wealth, incredible wisdom and unprecedented fame. As for sexual fulfilment, even 700 wives of royal birth and 300 concubines were not enough. He wanted more.

So many of God's servants do not finish life well owing to the inability to control their sexual desires. Billy Graham noted that it seems that the devil gets 75 per cent of God's best servants through sexual temptation. So many great men have fallen, and did not end well. As we saw early in this book, the Proverbs of Solomon plainly indicate that the lack of wisdom – folly – and sexual promiscuity go together. A person's genius is often the cause of his or her downfall. Solomon's answering all of the questions from the queen of Sheba may have convinced him all was well with him. But despite his wisdom, he let foreign wives compromise his greatness.

One would think that sexual lust is hardly a blind spot since it is so obvious. But in Solomon's case it began with what would seem to be a harmless allegiance to Pharaoh. Solomon even kept his Egyptian wife from the holy places (2 Chron. 8:11). This may have given him a 'pious' feeling that he was honouring God, but the devil had already won a victory. Marrying foreign women meant that Israel's downfall was only a matter of time.

Rehoboam

Rehoboam, the son of Solomon, had a vast and wealthy kingdom handed to him on a silver platter. The Israelite world lay at Rehoboam's feet. Never had a new king had it so easy! But Rehoboam – a man with a very insecure ego – had a blind spot. It was a rival spirit – he was jealous of his father.

The people of Israel came to Rehoboam with a request: 'Your father put a heavy yoke on us, but now lighten the harsh labour and the heavy yoke he put on us, and we will serve you' (1 Kings 12:4). The new king consulted with his elders, and these elders urged Rehoboam to give the people a favourable answer and they would 'always be your servants'. But sadly Rehoboam rejected the advice of his elders. His reply was: 'My father made your yoke heavy; I will make it even heavier. My father scourged you with whips; I will scourge you with scorpions' (v. 14). Rehoboam wanted all to know that 'my little finger is thicker than my father's waist' (v. 10). King Solomon's wisdom sadly was not passed on to the new king Rehoboam.

Rehoboam's utter lack of wisdom is typical of many leaders who feel a need to upstage their predecessor. They do not seem to grasp that this is Satan's trap. A new leader is often afraid that the people will prefer the previous leader, so Rehoboam wanted to prove he was stronger and greater than Solomon. How silly! But this pattern has been followed countless times. The greatest freedom is having nothing to prove. Rehoboam had no freedom. He was totally insecure and insanely jealous of his famous father's wisdom and fame. This led to the split of the kingdom of Israel. Things would never be the same again.

The thinking of John Calvin (1509–64)

Do you agree with John Calvin that in every saint there is something reprehensible? If so, do *you* admit to a blind spot? The irony is, if you could see past it, then it would no longer be a blind spot!

However, there are two kinds of blind spots – those you know about and those you don't. You might say that if one had a blind spot, he will be blind to his blind spot. Agreed! But it is none the less possible – by listening to loving and wise friends – to see your blind spot after all and accept their criticism and lessen the danger. On an everyday level, as I mentioned earlier, I know I need to be aware of a blind spot when driving my car – so I make sure another car has not come alongside me when I want to change lanes.

But there is also the unconscious blind spot. Take the theologian – and I call myself a theologian. I can be so convinced of my point of view that I become defensive and closed to a different point of view. I am sure I have many friends and foes who would quickly rush to tell me about some of my blind spots. But would I listen to them? I would try, but would they convince me? Who knows? Possibly not. I hate to say this, but I fear that only in heaven would I change some of my positions.

Did Calvin have a blind spot?

As for Calvin, a theological genius, I am personally convinced he too had a huge blind spot: his doctrine of the temporary faith of the reprobate. Reprobate (from the Greek *adokimos* – 'rejected') meant 'non-elect' to Calvin – namely, the person not chosen to salvation. Calvin's great wisdom failed him here. Calvin believed that the non-elect person may believe for a while and even show signs of sanctification. This teaching was embellished by the English Puritans and it became axiomatic for them and their followers. The result was that many Puritan preachers – not to mention their followers – had no real assurance that they were saved; they feared throughout their lives that they could be predestined to hell even though they had believed and had a change of life. They feared they were examples of the person not chosen, but who could have temporary faith. This is so unfortunate. *God wants us to know we are saved* if we have trusted the blood of his Son. We know we are saved by looking to Christ alone – putting all our eggs into one basket.

Calvin was inconsistent this time. On the one hand, he stressed that we should look to Christ alone to be saved – and be persuaded of our election to salvation. He even said that if we look to ourselves 'that is sure damnation'. On the other hand, his teaching that the non-elect could believe for a while kept people scared to death lest they be one of the non-elect with temporary faith, and therefore could not go to heaven. Looking to themselves – to see if they had sanctification – was precisely what the Puritans generally taught in order to know they were saved. The irony is, Calvin was against such introspection; he loathed the notion of a person looking to himself or herself to see whether he or she was saved. But his teaching of temporary faith of the non-elect inevitably invited the very introspection he was against. The sad result was that countless sincere believers never knew for sure whether they would go to heaven or hell. The origin of this way of thinking is traced to a theological blind spot in a great man. By the way, on his death bed Calvin summoned the pastors of Geneva to apologise for being bad-tempered with them.

Accountability

Most of all, I dread to think of a character flaw that everybody can see but me. I doubt not for a minute I have them. Perhaps many blind spots – too many to contemplate. For this reason I need to be accountable to people. Yes, *others*. As I said earlier in this book, the famous last words of yesterday's man or woman is 'I am accountable to *God alone*'. Strong leaders often say this: 'I am only accountable to God.' Wrong. I say to such a person, 'You aren't that spiritual.' Nobody is. We all need people around us who will tell us what our blind spots are – however painful it may be to hear about them: '. . . in an abundance of counselors there is safety' (Prov. 11:14, ESV). A flawed character is often the consequence of people who will not listen to their friends. Such people have become accountable to no one. Their downfall will certainly come.

When we know we have blind spots (e.g. the earlier example of me in my car) we can at least be on the lookout for a possible accident or tragedy. When we admit that we have unconscious character blind spots, it should keep us vulnerable and teachable – as much as possible. It is humbling to discover you have been wrong. Someone has to be wrong! It could be you. It could be me. 'No one is well fed until they have swallowed their pride and eaten their own words,' says Charles Carrin. May God grant that we lower our voices and be willing to wait for the time when the Lord steps in and shows us who got it right.

8

Concealed Wisdom

It is the glory of God to conceal
a matter. (Prov. 25:2)

No, we declare God's wisdom, a mystery
that has been hidden and that God destined
for our glory before time began. None of
the rulers of this age understood it, for if
they had, they would not have crucified
the Lord of glory. (1 Cor. 2:7–8)

Concealed wisdom is doing or saying something that makes no sense at the time, but which is in fact absolutely brilliant. This is God's style. He loves to do it. As a matter of fact, the biggest and deepest question in the history of the universe is 'Why does God allow evil and suffering when he could stop it?' It makes no sense to us. God has purposefully allowed the worst to be thought of him. For when he clears his name on the Final Day the world will be stunned. He saves the best for last. I say more about this in my book *Totally Forgiving God*.

In the meantime, God gives us bits and pieces of this kind of wisdom. It is the way he so often deals with his own – not revealing his reason for things, but requiring us to wait. Those who wait are richly rewarded. Those who are not prepared to wait never get the priceless treasure that could have been theirs.

The purpose of this chapter is to show why we should not find fault with the inexplicable things God does. Hold your breath; lower your voice; pause. All his works are done in faithfulness and truth (Ps. 33:4). He is looking for those who will trust him, rely on him, not give up. Without faith it is impossible to please him. Those who come to God must believe 'that he exists *and*' – don't forget the 'and' – that he 'rewards' those who seek him (Heb. 11:6). The reward is worth waiting for. His wisdom is worth pursuing. And if you don't know what is happening – and things don't make sense to you – trust him all the more. I guarantee: you will never be sorry.

Joseph and his silver cup in Benjamin's bag

If you have read my book *Total Forgiveness* you will know that I focus on the life of Joseph and how he forgave his brothers for the evil they did to him. But there is an episode in Joseph's life that many don't grasp – namely, why he hid his cup in Benjamin's bag – which appears to show that he hadn't forgiven them at all. When the eleven brothers came to Egypt to buy food they had to go to the prime minister – Joseph – but they had no idea it *was* Joseph. When Joseph sent the eleven brothers away with their bags full of corn he had his own silver cup placed in Benjamin's bag. Shortly after the brothers departed with their food, Joseph dispatched one of his officials to stop the eleven men and to accuse them of stealing the prime minister's silver cup. They were shocked, dumbfounded. The eleven brothers knew this could not possibly be true. They agreed that if indeed one of them had the silver cup he should die, and the rest remain the prime minister's slaves! But when they all emptied their bags, lo and behold, the prime minister's silver cup was in Benjamin's bag. 'At this, they tore their clothes. Then they all loaded their donkeys and returned to the city' (Gen. 44:13). When they faced the prime minister he questioned them sternly, asking how they could do such a thing. Joseph then said to them, 'Only the man who was found to have the cup will become my slave. The rest of you, go back to your father in peace' (Gen. 44:17).

Whatever was going on here? Was Joseph just having a little bit of fun with them, making them squirm? No. Was it a case of Joseph not having forgiven them after all, and he was rubbing their noses in it in an effort to get even? No. Was he trying to teach them a lesson to make sure they would never repeat their old offence again? No.

So why did Joseph do this? Answer: to prove that they were changed men. Joseph already knew how sorry they were; he knew how guilty they felt (Gen. 42:21–23). But there was a way of letting them *see for themselves* that they were different from how they were some twenty-two years before, when they planned to kill Joseph but instead agreed to sell him to the Ishmaelites.

If these men had not changed, they would have let Benjamin remain with Joseph – and headed on back to Canaan. They could have said, 'Sorry about that, Benjamin – goodbye.'

No. Judah came forward. He made what is possibly the most impassioned speech to be found in the entire Bible. No barrister ever provided a greater defence of a client in a courtroom. Read it – Genesis 44:18–34. Judah offers to stay behind himself, begging the prime minister to let him alone remain – and let the brothers go back to Canaan. He then not only pleads for Benjamin's life, but focuses on what it would do to their aged father if they came back to Canaan without Benjamin. Had they been looking for it, this was their chance to punish their dad for his callous lack of concern for their feelings. They had good reason to be bitter towards old Jacob, but they loved him despite him not being a loving father. 'So now,' Judah pleads with the apparently cold-hearted prime minister:

> If the boy [Benjamin] is not with us when I go back to your servant my father, and if my father, whose life is closely bound up with the boy's life, sees that the boy isn't there, he will die. Your servants will bring the grey head of our father down to the grave in sorrow . . . please let your servant remain here as my lord's slave in place

of the boy, and let the boy return with his brothers. How can I go back to my father if the boy is not with me? No! Do not let me see the misery that would come on my father (Gen. 44:30–34).

I doubt there was a dry eye in the house. Joseph himself broke down and sobbed – then revealed his identity to the eleven brothers, and demonstrated conclusively that he totally forgave them for all the evil they had done (Gen. 45:1–15).

In putting his silver cup in Benjamin's bag Joseph was actually showing his concern for his brothers. He told them, '. . . do not be distressed and do not be angry with your-selves' (Gen. 45:5), and he ensured this by letting them see they were *not the men they used to be*. It was a way of help-ing them to forgive themselves. God is like that. He not only forgives us for our folly, but wants us to forgive ourselves. When Joseph put his silver cup in Benjamin's bag it was a gracious set-up so the brothers could see they were decent, honourable men.

What Joseph did seemed heartless at first. Cruel. Mean. And had he never forgiven them for their evil act twenty-two years before, it would have made perfect sense. But he had forgiven them – and more: he wanted them to forgive themselves. It was a moving demonstration of total forgiveness.

God lets us save face by helping us to see we have truly changed. Not that we have become perfect – but better than we were. John Newton allegedly once said to his friend William Cowper: 'I'm not what I want to be. I'm not what I should be. I'm not what I hope to be. I'm not what I will be. But thank God I am not what I used to be.'

The brothers who were so evil twenty-two years before demonstrated – without knowing it was a set-up – that they were not what they used to be. The set-up gave them an opportunity to treat Benjamin, the only other son of Rachel, and now Jacob's favourite son, as they did Joseph. But instead of treating him as they treated Joseph, they stood firmly with Benjamin. They passed the test.

God does this all the time. He sets us up – doing things that make no sense at the time. It is wisdom concealed. And yet what God does actually makes himself look bad – for a while. But he can wait. His wisdom will be vindicated in the end.

If God is hiding his face from you, can you keep relying on him until things become clear? He deals with us only in wisdom and prudence (Eph. 1:8). He conceals his wisdom that you might trust him more and more – and discover for yourself that all he ever does is to love us.

Can you therefore wait for him to clear his name?

It is only a matter of time before you will see his wisdom in all he has done and allowed. He concealed his perfect wisdom – for a while.

The angel with a drawn sword

After the Israelites had spent forty years in the wilderness, Joshua, Moses' successor, led them into Canaan – the Promised Land. Soon after arriving, Joshua looked up and saw a man standing in front of them with a drawn sword in his hand. Joshua must have been impressed, if not intimidated. He asked, 'Are you for us or for our enemies?' The reply: 'Neither'. That was not what Joshua wanted to hear. '. . . as commander of the army of the LORD [meaning *Yahweh*] I have now come,' the angel continued. The impact was so overwhelming that Joshua fell face down on the ground in reverence. Joshua asked the angel, 'What message does my Lord have for his servant?' The reply was – much as Moses had been told long before – 'Take off your sandals, for the place where you are standing is holy ground.' And Joshua did this (Josh. 5:13–15; cf. Exod. 3:5).

The angel's comment that he was neither on the side of the children of Israel nor on the side of the inhabitants of Canaan – the very ones Joshua was commanded to conquer – was strange. It was about as mysterious as when God told Abraham to sacrifice Isaac, Isaac being the only link to the promise that God himself had given – namely, that Isaac's seed would be as numerous as the stars in the heavens (Gen. 22:1; Gen. 15:5). It made no sense.

May I ask you: are you perplexed at the moment with the way God is leading you? Does he appear to be contradicting himself? Does he seem not to be keeping his promise to you? I reply: congratulations. It may mean that God is dealing with you as he does his sovereign vessels. It is the way God dealt with Abraham – and all those listed in Hebrews 11 (those stalwarts who turned their world upside down by persistent faith). And it is the way God was dealing with Joshua.

Whatever was going on when the angel of the Lord – surely on the side of Israel – told Joshua he was on neither side? Was it really true? Was not the Lord actually on the side of his chosen people? If so, why did the angel tell Joshua something that was not true? Or was it true?

It was true. An angel's allegiance is always to God alone. No one else. All angels are *God's servants*. They serve us, yes, but only at God's pleasure. Their priority is to the Most High God – *their* Creator. Yes, angels are created beings; they exist not for us, but for him. All they do – ever – is to follow instructions.

So the angel told the absolute truth: that he was 'the commander of the army of the Lord'. Not only that; this was a very important angel. He was a high-ranking angel – the commander. The 'army' refers to countless angels who follow their commander. He will await instructions from the Lord God of the universe before he makes a move.

And yet there is more. The angel takes instructions from a God of glory. The true God is a God of glory. He does everything after the counsel of his own will (Eph. 1:11).

Joshua needed to learn a fundamental lesson about the true God: he has mercy on whom he will have mercy (Exod. 33:19; Rom. 9:15). This means no one has a claim on God. This would prohibit Joshua from developing a feeling of *entitlement* from God. With the angel responding as he did, Joshua would for ever and ever know his place and never be presumptuous. We can never snap our fingers at God and expect him to jump. We must always go to him on bended knee, asking for mercy (Heb. 4:16).

Does this surprise you? It may even disappoint you. I am sure it initially disappointed Joshua. But the Lord – *Yahweh* – wanted to know if Joshua would serve the Most High God for his being exactly as he is.

It was a set-up. God had sent this angel to see what Joshua's reaction would be. Joshua might have said to the angel – the commander of the Lord's army – 'Sorry. I will have nothing to do with you. I only want a God who puts me first in his heart. A God who will look after me. A God who will take care of me. A God who is on my side – who will defeat my enemies.'

God loves to challenge those whom he loves. When Abraham was ninety and Sarah was eighty – and barren – God said to Abraham, '. . . count the stars . . . so shall your offspring be' (Gen. 15:5). Abraham might have said, 'Do you really expect me to believe that? It is sheer nonsense. Leave me alone.' But no, Abraham believed the Lord. His faith was counted as righteousness (Gen. 15:6). When God told Abraham to sacrifice Isaac, he might have said, 'No.

You told me that Isaac was the promised child. I won't do that.' But Abraham tried to do it and God stepped in at the last minute and swore an oath to Abraham (Gen. 22:16).

God has a habit of testing our reaction to his surprising ways to see if we will love and worship him wholeheartedly when we discover more and more what the Lord God of Israel is really like. The true God – you will love him or hate him.

He is a God of glory; he is a jealous God. His name is Jealous (Exod. 34:14). This causes problems for some people; Oprah Winfrey has said that not understanding why God should be jealous led her to question her faith.

Behind the angel's word to Joshua was concealed wisdom. It was in Joshua's own interest that he should learn more about God than he knew at the time. Why? Because Joshua would need a lot of wisdom from now on – wisdom he did not have. The only way to true wisdom is to know the ways of the Lord. Joshua may have felt betrayed at first when the angel with the drawn sword spoke as he did. But when the angel said he was the commander of the army of the Lord – *Yahweh* – that was good enough for Joshua. He fell face down and worshipped. He gladly took off his sandals. He knew he was on holy ground.

Which is more important to you: having a God who merely looks after you – and nothing more – or *knowing* this God who looks after you? The Lord wanted to see if Joshua was interested in knowing him rather than merely having a God who will fight his battles.

Yes, God instructed the angel to reply as he did for Joshua's sake. This concealed wisdom was about Joshua's deepest concern after all! God only wants what is best for us. He would do Joshua no favours merely by saying, 'I'm on your side.' That would have been impersonal, distant, detached; a remote – if not a cold – reply. God is not like that. He wants us to know him. He wants to see if we will worship him when he unfolds more and more of himself. But it comes with a challenge – as with Abraham, Isaac and Jacob and all of God's esteemed servants. God treats you with highest dignity when he appears to betray you. It means you have been upgraded to the Big League. Martin Luther always said you must know God as an enemy before you can know him as a friend.

I certainly don't want to be unfair, but I have a fear that many Christians today don't have a clue as to the nature of the God of the Bible. The superficiality in much of the modern Church is so widespread.

It is possible too that the angel was saying to Joshua, 'I have not come to take sides, I have come to take over.' It was fair enough if that too was implied in the reply that initially surprised Joshua. For the commander of the Lord's army wants to be in control – you can be sure of that!

All that was entailed in the reply Joshua received is what fitted him to be Moses' successor in the Promised Land. Joshua was given a glimpse of the God who promised to be with him as he had been with Moses (Josh. 1:5). Moses' most earnest request to God was, 'Show me your ways'

(Exod. 33:13). If Joshua was going to be a fit successor to Moses, he had to know God's ways. Knowing God's ways is what leads to true wisdom. There are no short-cuts. God was treating Joshua exactly as he had dealt with Moses. He could receive no higher compliment than that. And if God treats you as he did Moses and Joshua, you can receive no higher compliment.

The strange ways of Mordecai

The book of Esther is mainly about Mordecai the Jew. Mordecai adopted his cousin Esther because she had no living parents. Because of her beauty she was chosen by King Ahasuerus to be the next Queen. But Mordecai instructed her not to reveal her Jewish identity. They were ever conscious that they lived in a country that hated Jews.

King Ahasuerus promoted Haman the Agagite by 'elevating him and giving him a seat of honour higher than that of all the other nobles. All the royal officials at the king's gate knelt down and paid honour to Haman, for the king had commanded this concerning him' (Esther 3:1–2). This was much like King Nebuchadnezzar requiring everyone to bow to the golden image he had set up (Dan. 3:1–7).

But Mordecai did not kneel down or pay him honour. The king's servants asked Mordecai, 'Why do you disobey the king's command?' Mordecai would not answer them – though they asked him day after day. They then told Haman that Mordecai the Jew refused to pay him honour. They wanted to see whether Haman would let Mordecai off the hook. Not a chance! Haman was 'enraged' (Esther 3:5), but he decided to do nothing at first to get even with Mordecai.

Haman had a far more sinister and far-reaching plan. Instead of punishing Mordecai alone, Haman decided to destroy *all* the Jews throughout the entire kingdom of Ahasuerus. Haman went to the king. He told the king nothing about Mordecai's behaviour, but made the claim that the Jews in the land were disloyal and must be exterminated. He managed to get the king to swear an oath that could never be rescinded which gave Haman the right to get rid of all Jews.

All this was the result of Mordecai's curious passive behaviour – refusing to pay honour to Haman.

Whatever was Mordecai thinking? Didn't he know this would get him – if not all Jews – into trouble? He actually appeared rude. Mordecai's personal refusal to show Haman reverence thus meant that all Jews would be slaughtered. Therefore what Mordecai did made no sense at all. It was surely the most imprudent and counterproductive act he could possibly have conceived.

And yet it was concealed wisdom, but this wisdom was concealed even from Mordecai himself. Whereas he knew exactly what he was doing – sticking to his guns by not showing reverence to Haman – he still did not realise it would cause the horrific stir that it did. He did not view his actions as shrewd or anything that might be ultimately advantageous for his people the Jews. In other words, Mordecai had no secret plan in mind in his refusal to bow to Haman.

But God did. The wisdom that lay behind Mordecai's disrespectful act was not Mordecai trying to be brilliant. He had no idea how things would turn out. But behind all the strange actions of Mordecai lay divine wisdom and love for God's chosen people. A further irony in all this is that the name of God is never mentioned at all in the book of Esther.

Mordecai was not only willing to be misunderstood and appear strange to everybody – including Esther – but he was prepared to die.

What motivated Mordecai's behaviour? First, *a Jew bows down only to Yahweh*. Simple as that. Mordecai risked his very life in order to uphold the true worship of God. He was obeying the First Commandment: 'You shall have no other gods before me' (Exod. 20:3). To Mordecai, bowing down to Haman was tantamount to idolatry. Second, *God would honour Mordecai's loyal adherence* to the First Commandment. The eventual result would make Mordecai a hero to Jews for all time, but Mordecai had no idea this would happen.

And yet this behaviour would have taken exceedingly rare courage. When Haman's plan was announced – that all Jews would be slaughtered on a set date – Mordecai got Queen Esther's attention by tearing off his clothes and putting on sackcloth and ashes, and going out into the city 'wailing loudly and bitterly' (Esther 4:1). He sent word to her of Haman's plan to kill every single Jew. Mordecai knew that the only link to the future of the Jews lay with Esther. He then put this proposition to her: '. . . who knows but that you have come to your royal position for such a time as this?' (Esther 4:14). She then agreed to approach the king at great risk to her own life. 'And if I perish, I perish,' she said in her decision to get the king's attention (Esther 4:16).

Please read the book of Esther for the rest of the amazing details. In short, in an extraordinary sudden turn-around of events and coincidences, the king not only showed favour to Esther but had Haman hung on the gallows he had prepared for Mordecai! They also managed to work around the king's oath in a manner that spared all the Jews – namely, giving all Jews the right to defend themselves. They were miraculously spared.

Do you think you could be a Mordecai? What if people saw you as exceedingly strange? And then how would you feel if you found out – to your great surprise and amazement – that you were a strategic part of God's plan for his people when all you did was to be faithful to the Lord? You were not conscious of any great wisdom or doing any great deed. In fact, people questioned your wisdom! They didn't understand what it was you were doing! What if they questioned your faith and integrity? And then, eventually, it turned out that you were exonerated and totally vindicated? You could only say 'I have only done my duty', as Jesus put it in Luke 17:10. Boasting is not allowed!

Mordecai had no idea he was a vital part of God's plan for his people. All he did was to stick to his conviction about the true God. He had obviously been taught well. He could not have known he was the very next step forward for what God wanted to do for his people. Things got worse before they got better! But God is never too early, never too late; he's always just on time! Mordecai's stance was the equivalent of what three Hebrews – Shadrach, Meshach and Abednego – did when they refused to bow to the golden image that King Nebuchadnezzar had set up (Dan. 3:16–18). They were not going to bow even if God appeared to desert them! They said to the king, 'Our God is able to deliver us.' Yes. *But if not*, 'be it known to you, O king, that we will not serve your gods or worship the golden image that you have set up' (Dan. 3:17–18, ESV).

Do you have the 'but if not' faith?

The Virgin Mary

The angel Gabriel went to a teenage girl in Nazareth with startling news: 'You will conceive and give birth to a son, and you are to call him Jesus.' Mary replied, 'How will this be . . . since I am a virgin?' The angel assured her that the Holy Spirit would come upon her, and that the power of the Holy Spirit would overshadow her 'so the holy one to be born will be called the Son of God' (Luke 1:31, 34–35). Her instant wisdom set in: 'I am the Lord's servant . . . May your word to me be fulfilled' (Luke 1:38). Immediately after that, Mary became pregnant with the Son of God.

In her wisdom she kept absolutely quiet about all this, knowing she would be looked upon with extreme disgrace. She shared the news only with her cousin Elizabeth. But her ultimate wisdom was keeping quiet about this event until many years later. We won't know the details until we get to heaven, but it is apparent that Mary told nobody of the virgin birth of Jesus until she shared it with Luke a genera-tion later (Luke 2:51).

The crucifixion of Jesus

There are two important theological issues that lie behind this chapter. First, does Satan know the future? Answer: no. The proof of this is that he would not have engineered the crucifixion of Jesus had he known what it would mean. The wisdom of God was withheld from the devil or the princes of this world 'would not have crucified the Lord of glory' (1 Cor. 2:8). The devil had no idea that the crucifix-ion was God's idea and that it was in fact what guaranteed Satan's defeat. This leads to the second theological issue: who crucified Jesus? Was it the Romans? The Jews? Satan? God? Answer: all of these. A solid case can be made that Pontius Pilate is really responsible for Jesus' crucifixion, and yet Pilate would never have carried it out had not the Jews demanded it of him. That said, Satan entered Judas

Iscariot (John 13:2) who betrayed Jesus. This shows that the devil thought he masterminded the crucifixion. But the clear teaching of the Bible is that God himself was at the bottom of it all. It pleased the Lord to crush him (Isa. 53:10). On the day of Pentecost Peter preached that Jesus was turned over to the authorities by 'God's set purpose and foreknowledge' (Acts 2:23). The Romans and Jews 'did what your power and will had decided beforehand should happen' (Acts 4:28). So at the end of the day God takes the responsibility for Jesus' crucifixion. The reason Jesus came into the world in the first place was to die on a cross!

And yet there is someone else who crucified Jesus – for it must be said that you and I crucified Jesus.

> *Was it for crimes that I had done He groaned upon*
> *the tree?*
> *Amazing pity, grace unknown, and love beyond*
> *degree.*
>
> Isaac Watts, (1664–1748)

> *I saw my sins His blood had spilt.*
>
> John Newton, (1725–1807)

If you were in Jerusalem on Good Friday 2,000 years ago and asked, 'What is God doing in Jerusalem today?', the reply would have been: 'It's Passover, we are going to celebrate the way God delivered the children of Israel from Pharaoh's bondage – that is, if that awful, horrible thing hanging on a cross outside the city would hurry up and die.'

There is the old spiritual, 'Were you there when they crucified my Lord?' I ask: what do you suppose you would have seen, thought or felt had you been physically present at the place called Golgotha when Jesus was hanging on the cross?

Not a single person in Jerusalem had a clue as to what was happening when Jesus died on that cross. Not one soul.

Those most mystified by the event were the followers of Jesus. They could not figure it out. How could someone who raised Lazarus from the dead let Roman soldiers crucify him? How could someone who could walk on water not stop this awful thing? Jesus himself said he could call a legion of angels at any moment to rescue him from the wickedness of the men who brought about the crucifixion (Matt. 26:53).

The two men on the road to Emmaus after Jesus' resurrection expressed what the followers of Jesus had thought to be true: 'We thought he would redeem Israel . . .' Uppermost on the disciples' minds was an earthly kingdom Jesus would set up – and overthrow Rome (Acts 1:6).

Mind you, his followers ought not to have been surprised. First, Jesus predicted his crucifixion (Matt. 16:21; Luke 18:32). This word somehow leaked out because some Jews warned Pilate that Jesus might be raised from the dead; therefore Pilate ordered that the tomb be secured (Matt. 27:62–66). In other words, Jesus clearly predicted that he would be crucified. Second, Jesus taught that his kingdom was not of this world; it was not a visible thing, but rather a spiritual kingdom (Luke 17:20–21).

Nothing added up for those disciples who were closest to him – but it should have. When Jesus spoke of a kingdom within – or of a crucifixion – his words went right past the Twelve. It was not what they wanted to hear, so they 'heard nothing' that went against their deepest hopes.

Everyone had their hopes up on Palm Sunday. The crowds shouted 'Hosanna!' All believed the Great Moment had finally arrived. But on Good Friday their hopes were dashed. Judas Iscariot had betrayed Jesus, and the authorities had taken Jesus into custody. Not only did Simon Peter deny knowing Jesus; in fact, all the disciples forsook him and fled (Matt. 26:56).

As people who were aware of his miracles gazed upon the crucified one, some hoped – even now – that he would come down from the cross as the soldier challenged him to do (Matt. 27:40). Perhaps Mary Magdalene hoped right to the end that Jesus would defy everybody and come down from the cross in irresistible power. But, as we know, instead he died.

It was concealed wisdom. The crucifixion of Jesus was in fact the greatest display of concealed wisdom that ever was. True wisdom is God's secret, and this was the best-kept secret from the beginning of time. The crucifixion was God's secret plan to do several things in just a few hours: (1) defeat death; (2) defeat the devil; (3) fulfil the Law; (4) atone for sin; (5) fulfil Scripture. In one stroke God took everyone by surprise; the crucifixion was God's way of saving the world. The blood of Jesus simultaneously atoned for sin and turned God's wrath away from the world, for God was in Christ reconciling the world to himself (2 Cor. 5:19).

When you consider that the crucifixion of Jesus was the greatest thing in world history since creation – and no one understood it at the time – how much more could lesser events be misunderstood too? God himself takes the responsibility for being misunderstood for a while, knowing his name will be cleared down the line. Could it be, then, that you are going through a difficult time at the moment which makes no sense – but God is none the less at the bottom of it all? He will make things clear to you in his time. He knows the plans he has for you – to bless and prosper you (Jer. 29:11)!

Paul's wisdom and the gospel

The apostle Paul stated that he made a calculated decision before he went to Corinth: 'For I resolved to know nothing while I was with you except Jesus Christ and him crucified' (1 Cor. 2:2). The ancient Greeks knew what a crucifixion was. The capital punishment in the Graeco-Roman world was reserved for the most vile and worst criminals. Horrible and painful though the crucifixion was, no one felt sorry for those who received this punishment. Not only that, but the stigma attached to a Roman crucifixion was such that for Paul to have made this decision to know nothing among them but Christ and him crucified would seem very unwise indeed. Preposterous. It was surely the most imprudent way forward to impress these Greeks. It could even be said that if Paul wanted to come up with the very kind of talk that would alienate the people of Corinth he could not do better than to preach Jesus Christ crucified!

To put it another way, had Paul hired a public relations expert to open doors in Corinth, he might have said, 'If you want to get converts to Christianity, announce that Jesus heals and that you are going to pray for the sick.' Or 'Promise people prosperity if they come to Jesus'. Or 'Tell them that prophetic words will be spoken over them. You need to find an entry point, Paul, if you are going to reach these people. Whatever, don't mention crucifixion in connection with your message.' But Paul had already made up his mind: he would give the people of Corinth nothing but Jesus Christ and 'him crucified'.

Whatever was Paul thinking? It was concealed wisdom. But such wisdom was not concealed to Paul himself. It was clear to him. After all, he only wanted to see people saved in Corinth. Converted; spared from the coming wrath of God. And he knew one other thing: no one would be converted apart from the Holy Spirit drawing them. Jesus said that no one 'can' – that is, no one is *able* – to come to him unless the Father draws him. This was a reference to the Holy Spirit. In other words, in order to get people saved it was necessary to get the Holy Spirit involved. And there is one thing that guarantees that the Holy Spirit will get involved – namely, talking about Jesus Christ and the blood he shed on the cross. That gets the Holy Spirit's attention. Paul needed the Holy Spirit. Without the Spirit he would utterly fail; with the Spirit he would succeed. The mention of crucifixion may not appeal to the wisdom of this world, but Paul wasn't representing worldly wisdom in the first place. He was there to preach the gospel.

Furthermore, a person can never be saved until he hears that Jesus died on the cross – and why. Paul knew he had to bring in the death of Jesus in order to see people saved. So why postpone mentioning this? Why precede the preaching of the gospel with a lot of stuff that appeals to the flesh? Paul's rationale is to get the Holy Spirit involved as soon as possible, so 'let's begin and end with Jesus Christ and him crucified'. That is the way his mind worked.

However, knowing 'Christ and him crucified' may be understood in two ways: (1) the content of the sermon or message; and (2) exemplifying Jesus Christ who submitted to the cross. The primary meaning is the gospel message. But Paul also made a calculated decision to show the Corinthians the type of man Jesus himself was. Paul was going to emulate Jesus. He was prepared to be like Jesus; to live like Jesus; to be unpretentious like Jesus; to turn the other cheek like Jesus; to forgive like Jesus; to mingle with sinners as Jesus did; to accept people like Jesus would. Paul reckoned that if he lived like that, the Corinthians would want what he had – and would listen to anything he would say.

To put it another way, if Paul went into Corinth depending only on his sermons – however sound in explaining what Jesus did on the cross – and did not demonstrate the humility and attitude of Jesus by his personal life, the Holy Spirit might not get involved so quickly in his ministry. Paul wanted to be sound doctrinally, yes; he equally wanted his life among the Corinthians to make an impact so that his hearers would see selfless love, transparency and integrity that would compel them to want to come to Christ.

Did it work? It certainly did! Hundreds and hundreds were saved – 1 and 2 Corinthians form the largest corpus of New Testament letters devoted to one church (and two other letters were lost). Yes, Paul's wisdom worked.

The only true wisdom is God's wisdom. That is what gripped Paul and convinced him to adopt the stance of knowing nothing but Christ crucified. He believed it so much that he was willing to be misunderstood. He wasn't looking for instant vindication of his decision. He wanted to be in partnership with the Holy Spirit. That is wisdom.

Arthur Blessitt

For my last illustration of concealed wisdom I have chosen to go outside biblical history in order to focus on one of the most unusual, daring, original and charismatic figures I have ever met. If Hebrews 11 were extended to the present time, I reckon Arthur Blessitt would be included. I referred to him earlier in this book. He was a leading figure of the Jesus Movement that sprung up in California in the 1960s. After attending Mississippi College he went to Golden Gate Theological Seminary for a while, but preferred to witness in the streets of San Francisco. He then left for Elko, Nevada, and started a church (still in existence). He moved to California and opened a coffee shop called His Place in Hollywood's Sunset Strip. He constructed a twelve-foot wooden cross and put it on the wall of His Place so those who came in would understand why only coffee and orange juice were available. (He later observed, 'If I knew I was going to carry it I wouldn't have made it so big.') He used His Place as a platform to preach the gospel. All was going well – except for one thing. His Place was located next door to a strip club and the owners of the building (who owned the premises for both the strip club and Arthur's coffee shop) ejected Arthur because he was adversely affecting the strip club's business. Arthur and his followers were constantly leading people to Christ right, left and centre – especially if they came near His Place.

Arthur began a fast and chained himself to his cross on the pavement outside His Place to protest against his unlawful ejection. Within two weeks of his fast, the newspapers picked up on it and made the 'Jesus freak' both local and national news overnight. When his friend Dr Jess Moody, then pastor of First Baptist Church of West Palm Beach,

Florida, saw this in the news he flew to Los Angeles. He was convinced that Arthur had either lost his mind or at best had gone off the rails. He said to Arthur, 'Whatever are you doing? Are you crazy? Why are you doing this? What do you expect to accomplish?' Arthur looked at Jess and said, 'Jess, I have nowhere to go. My ministry to witness for Jesus is all I have.' In the meantime people were coming from all over Los Angeles to see this weird sight chained to his cross. Arthur took full advantage of this, witnessing to all who talked to him and leading many to Christ – including some well-known film stars. In the meantime Jess used some of his contacts in the Los Angeles area to help Arthur. A group of Black Panthers soon came along, and walked upstairs over His Place to talk to the owner of the building. They asked what Arthur had done wrong – had he not paid his rent? That was not the problem, the owner said; Arthur was hurting his trade at the strip club. These Black Panthers cautioned the owner that if he did not let Arthur back inside His Place there could be a riot in the streets. Arthur was given a different venue down the street, and was back in the new location of His Place immediately, but was by now a national figure – in some ways, he was a tourist attraction!

In the autumn of 1969 Jess Moody arranged for Arthur to speak to the Southern Baptists of South Florida. I was then pastor of the Lauderdale Manors Baptist Church in Fort Lauderdale. When I heard Arthur speak, I was stunned and amazed – but thrilled. I was allowed to spend a few minutes with him, and I brought Louise to meet him a couple of hours later. His first words to her were, 'Are you saved?'

Jess Moody later shared something with me. 'Arthur's done it again, R.T., you won't believe what he is going to do now.' Praying at five o'clock in the morning (not because he got up early but because he had been praying all night), 'Arthur says the Lord told him to take the cross down from the wall at His Place and carry it on foot around the world.' Jess added that there would be no way to stop him.

Arthur planned to begin his walk across the USA on Christmas Day – 25 December 1969. However, two weeks before this he developed an aneurism (blood clot) on his brain. His doctors told him not to move – not even to think of trying to leave the hospital. But Arthur said, 'The Lord told me to carry the cross. I made the commitment. Circumstances don't change the commitment.' He began his walk on schedule.

He carried the cross on foot, averaging some five to fifteen miles per day. A typical pattern was this. When he would come to a town the local newspaper would have him photographed, and put his picture on the front page. People would come out to see this strange man who was presenting the gospel to them. People would pray the 'sinner's prayer' with him and Arthur would go to the next town. That scenario was repeated countless times. When he came to Columbus, Ohio, Phil Roberts went to hear him. Arthur's ministry led Phil to surrender to the call of God to preach.

Phil then went to Southern Baptist Theological Seminary in Louisville, Kentucky (I was a student with him), later got his doctorate from the Free University of Amsterdam, and eventually became president of Midwestern Baptist Theological Seminary in Kansas City, Missouri.

We will not know until we get to heaven how many people Arthur Blessitt has led to Jesus Christ on a one-to-one basis. If I were to give an honest estimate I would say tens and tens of thousands, not counting those who responded to his public preaching. He crossed the USA in about eight months, ending in Washington, DC. Then he went to the UK, followed by Europe and Africa. He went to the Middle East in 1977. While in Israel in 1980 he met and spent time with Yasser Arafat – and again with Arafat in Beirut, Lebanon, in 1982. He was given the Sinai Peace Medal in 1980 when he walked from Jerusalem to Cairo. He stayed in the home of Israel's then prime minister, Menachim Begin. Not that this was a prize he particularly sought, but he has been given the *Guinness Book of Records* award for the 'longest walk' – over 40,500 miles (equivalent of once and a half around the world). Has walked in literally every sovereign country and in every major inhabited island group in the world. Total: 321 nations, island groups and territories. He walked across the Sahara Desert in several stages in the late 1980s.

While at Westminster Chapel I was president of the Fellowship of Independent Evangelical Churches – a very conservative group. When I suggested they have Arthur

Blessitt to preach at their annual meeting they thought I was joking. It took three committee meetings to get it through, but Arthur addressed their gathering with the Chapel filled from top to bottom. His subject: 'Do we still need the cross?' Many people came to the Lord that night, including Beryl Grogan, who would become my secretary several years later. I mentioned earlier in the book that I invited Arthur to stay at the Chapel for a while – six Sunday evenings in April–May 1982. During that period our daughter Melissa was saved.

Arthur has written several books. He wrote the Foreword to the US edition of my book *Did You Think to Pray?* Arthur is a man of prayer about as much as anybody I have ever known. He always signs Luke 18:1 to his name ('they should always pray and not give up'). A film about his life was recently made – called *The Cross* – and was first launched at the Grauman's Chinese Theatre in Hollywood. He still carries the cross as much as he can. He now has a mild heart condition that prohibits him from being in the sun for very long. The aneurism is still there! He now regularly hosts programmes on Trinity Broadcasting Network (TBN). The welcoming open doors now given to him at the age of seventy-two are phenomenal. He carries the cross every morning in his neighbourhood in Denver, Colorado. People in cars line up or to watch him, and roll down their windows as he talks about Jesus and – when possible – leads people to the Lord.

I close this chapter with what will always be a part of my own testimony from now on. I am amazed I had not thought of this before. While being interviewed by Arthur recently on TBN, I reminded him that I once asked that his mantle – or anointing – fall on me. It was a cheeky request, but I did ask. He remembered it well. On our knees together in my vestry at Westminster Chapel he laid his hands on me and prayed that God would answer my request. During this television interview I asked, 'Was that prayer answered?' I suddenly thought to ask that. Why not before? I don't know. Until that moment I had never paused to ask the question as to whether Arthur's prayer for his anointing to be passed on to me was answered. It is a request that goes back to May 1982 – over thirty years ago. So was that prayer answered?

Yes – it hit me for the first time. On a Friday night in May 1982, when Arthur was witnessing to every person who came along on Buckingham Gate, he turned to me and said, 'You don't need to leave the steps of your church. You have the whole world here.' In that moment I had a vision (or something like that) of a pilot light – a light that stays lit day and night in a cooker or oven. The Pilot Light ministry was born. My ambitions, plans and wishes to be a great theologian lay at Jesus' feet in ashes that night. I knew I was to be an evangelist from that moment, and that is exactly what I became from that night. An evangelist. I still am. Almost wherever I go – on planes, in taxis, in restaurants. So it hit me: YES, that prayer was answered. I have never been the same since Arthur Blessitt came into my life. I simply had not connected it to his prayer for me. Call it

what you wish – mantle, anointing or a burning commitment to talk to people everywhere, not merely from a pulpit
(which is easier than talking to strangers), about Jesus
Christ. I am not Arthur. But that prayer was answered.

Like all those people described in Hebrews 11, Arthur is
not perfect. But he is one of the most unusual – and under-
estimated – men I have met. In fact, he reminds me a bit of
Mordecai.

9

How to Get the Mind
of the Holy Spirit

I saw the Spirit come down from heaven as
a dove and remain on him. (John 1:32)

After the festival was over, while his
parents were returning home, the boy
Jesus stayed behind in Jerusalem, but
they were unaware of it. (Luke 2:43)

When I was at Westminster Chapel, I always began my
Sunday morning sermon preparation on Monday
mornings. There was one exception in twenty-five years –
only one – when I found myself unprepared on a Saturday
morning. I prayed that there would be no interruptions all
day and that God would overrule my unpreparedness (it
had been a busy week – no time to prepare a sermon) and
come to my aid. At 9 a.m. that day Louise and I had a bad
argument. I slammed the door and went to my study. I
opened my Bible and asked the Lord to help me write my
sermon. At 11 a.m. all I had was a blank sheet of paper.

Nothing came. I began to panic. 'Lord, please', I prayed, 'help me'. By 1 p.m. – nothing; 2 p.m. – nothing. 'Lord, please, please help me – what I say tomorrow will be tape recorded and heard all over the world' – still nothing but a blank sheet of paper and my Bible. However, at 4 p.m. I knew what I had to do. It hurt a bit. I went to the kitchen; there was Louise standing by the fridge, tearful. I said, 'Honey, I am so sorry. It's all my fault.' 'Well, it was partly my fault too,' she replied kindly. 'No. It was all my fault and I am so sorry.' We kissed; we hugged. I went back to my study to my Bible and blank sheet of paper.

I can tell you, in forty-five minutes I literally had all I needed for my Sunday morning sermon. Before 5 p.m. the sermon was ready. Why? The Dove came down. I had the mind of the Spirit. My sermon the following Sunday morning was possibly the best I had preached since arriving at the Chapel many years before.

You can accomplish more in five minutes when the Holy Spirit comes down than you can in five years when you try to do things in your own strength.

However, I need to make one other thing clear: I refer to the immediate and direct witness of the Holy Spirit. This is the Holy Spirit's own witness – literally knowing you are hearing directly from God. But don't we hear from God by reading the Bible? Yes, of course. Absolutely. But the Holy Spirit also wants to come to us immediately, directly. So when I refer to the presence of the mind of the Spirit I mean hearing God directly. It will *always* cohere with Holy

Scripture – be sure of that. But it is none the less a direct witness, not unlike when the Holy Spirit spoke directly to Philip (Acts 8:26–39).

Wisdom is having the presence of the mind of the Holy Spirit – not mere presence of mind. As we saw in Chapter 2, common grace comes to non-Christians non-stop, often issuing in presence of mind – that is, unusual strength and peace. But the presence of the mind of the Holy Spirit is granted to Christians who have not grieved the Spirit.

The presence of the mind of the Holy Spirit is of course to have the mind of the Most High God from whom all wisdom proceeds. The degree to which we have the mind of the Spirit will be the degree to which we grasp *exactly* what to do and say.

The greatest challenge I have ever been faced with in my entire life is *how not to grieve the Holy Spirit*. Nothing is more challenging than this. I am conscious of this every day. It is because grieving the Holy Spirit is the easiest thing in the world to do. Like it or not, the Holy Spirit is a very, very sensitive person. When I wrote the book *Sensitivity of the Spirit* I actually wanted to all it 'Hyper-Sensitivity of the Spirit', but my publisher (wisely) talked me out of it. But that does get the point over – the Holy Spirit is hyper-sensitive. Now when we speak of a person being 'hyper-sensitive' it is not a compliment. But that is the way the Holy Spirit is! He is *so* sensitive. When Paul said for us not to 'grieve' the Holy Spirit (Eph. 4:30) he used a Greek word that means to have your feelings hurt. The Holy Spirit has feelings and these feelings get hurt easily. Why is this? I cannot be sure. The best answer I have is that the Holy Spirit has apparently deigned to relate to our finiteness so we can learn what he is like and discover our own sin by grieving him. You may say, 'He ought not to be like that.' But that is the way he *is* and he is the only Holy Spirit you've got!

The Holy Spirit is depicted in the New Testament as a dove. The dove is a very shy, sensitive bird. I have a close friend in Ada, Oklahoma, called Pete Cantrell, and he is arguably one of the top authorities on pigeons and doves. He has studied them all his life. He explained to me that a dove is basically a wild bird. 'You can train a pigeon,' he said to me, 'but you cannot train a dove.' Pigeons are boisterous, belligerent and unafraid of people. Doves are gentle and loving, but afraid of people.

A dove is shy and sensitive, but the Holy Spirit is a thousand times more sensitive than a dove.

So how do we find the mind of the Holy Spirit? I list four things below that will likely bring about the presence of the mind of the Holy Spirit.

1 Find out what grieves the Spirit – and avoid doing it

John the Baptist was given a clue as to how to recognise the Messiah. He was told to watch for when the Holy Spirit would come down 'as a dove *and remain* on him' (John 1:32 – my italics). Note the word 'remain'. I know what it is for the Holy Spirit to come down on me. Yes – for a moment or two. But he does not *remain*. He does not stay long. Why? Because I will inevitably and invariably do or say something that grieves him, and he, as it were, flies away. It may be when I am impatient with a slow car in front of me. It may be in a supermarket when I am in a hurry and the person in front of me at the till is slowly counting his or her change – and I breathe heavily (wanting to be heard). It may be when I say a cross word to my wife. I grieve the Holy Spirit when I say unflattering things about someone. I absolutely grieve the Spirit when I hold a grudge and will not forgive. Indeed, the first thing Paul says to the reader, having said not to grieve the Holy Spirit, is: 'Get rid of all bitterness, rage and anger, brawling and slander, along with every form of malice. Be kind and compassionate to one another, forgiving each other, just as in Christ God forgave you' (Eph. 4:31–32).

What exactly happens when I grieve the Holy Spirit? There is good news and bad news. The good news is that I do not lose my salvation. Paul said, '. . . do not grieve the Holy Spirit of God, with whom you were *sealed for the day of redemption*' (Eph. 4:30 – my italics). Nothing could be clearer than that! So at least I know I have not lost my salvation. But the bad news is that I lose the *presence of the mind* of the Holy Spirit. I don't lose the Holy Spirit himself; he abides with me for ever (John 14:17). But I lose the anointing by which the mind of God is conveyed to me. It is as though the Dove lifts – flies away. It is a metaphor of course, but the point is that I lose the knowledge of what to do and what to say when I grieve the Holy Spirit. That is what happened to me when I had that terrible row with Louise before I tried to write my sermon.

The Holy Spirit will not bend the rules for any of us. It does not matter how old or mature you are, what your profile is – whether you are a deacon or pastor; how well you know the Bible; whether you are a new Christian or a seasoned theologian. The Holy Spirit does not adjust to us. We have to adjust to him. That is why I had to apologise to Louise if I wanted to hear from God.

When I write a sermon I do my best to hear God. I don't read commentaries – at least not at first. I may not read them at all if I am happy with what I have prepared. I only consult commentaries on extremely difficult verses or when I want to be sure I have not gone off the deep end! In order to prepare sermons in this manner, I of necessity have to be on guard regarding my personal life.

It cannot be exaggerated how easy it is to grieve the Holy Spirit, and one of the chief ways we do this is by bitterness, anger and unforgiveness – in other words, holding a grudge. It is therefore absolutely essential that my relationship with Louise is such that I can hear God speak when I prepare a sermon. Otherwise I will have to go and read a book or borrow from another preacher's sermon – but I forfeit saying anything that is *fresh*, which of course is what people want when they listen to a minister.

Do I always succeed? Of course not. Does the indwelling ungrieved Spirit make me perfect? Don't make the angels laugh. All of us have the Spirit in measure, but only Jesus had the Spirit without any limit (John 3:34). But a little bit of the Spirit – when he is ungrieved in me – is sufficient to help me know what to say, and what not to say.

The bottom line is: when I preach I want the wisdom of the Holy Spirit, not the wisdom of a biblical commentary (however erudite or orthodox). In order to have the Spirit's wisdom it means my own spirit must be at peace. When this is the case I am more likely to hear from God. When I am not at peace with myself, or with anybody else, I find it virtually impossible to prepare a sermon – or to know what to say or do next.

Perhaps the most common problem is to run ahead of the Lord, thinking the whole time that he was right there with you. To run ahead of God is an easy thing to do – Joseph and Mary did it. They walked ten or fifteen miles without their little boy, but thought the entire time that he was with them. They were wrong – and were extremely distraught that this could happen.

You and I must develop the kind of relationship with the Lord whereby we know he is walking with us – that we are certain we are not running ahead of him, and would be distraught should this happen. We won't do it perfectly; it takes practice. I have a little book I recommend – *The Practice of the Presence of God* – by a man called Brother Lawrence, a French Catholic monk. He speaks candidly of his unusual relationship with Jesus Christ. The fact that such a book could be called 'practice' of the presence of

God is a fairly clear hint that we are all aiming for this. We practise the presence of God. We practise having the mind of the Holy Spirit. None of us completely arrive; none of us will have the Holy Spirit without measure or limit.

But one thing is for sure: we must avoid any bitterness, holding a grudge, not forgiving those who hurt us. And when you are angry? Admit your folly, climb down, and repent. If you ran ahead of the Lord and finding your way back to where Jesus is calls for you to apologise, then do it. There is nothing comparable to the awareness of the ungrieved Spirit. This is the source of the wisdom we need – whether it be preparing sermons or knowing what to say or do next.

2 Controlling the tongue

Shortly after encouraging us to ask God for wisdom if we lack it (Jas. 1:5), James turns to the issue of controlling the tongue. The first reference to this is when James said, '. . . everyone should be quick to listen, slow to speak and slow to become angry' (Jas. 1:19). If we are slow to speak we are less likely to become openly angry. One of the best words of advice I ever heard was when Dr Martyn Lloyd-Jones said to me, 'When you are agitated, don't speak.' But when we are agitated and also speak, it is much like the spark that causes a forest fire, as James says later on: 'Consider what a great forest is set on fire by a small spark' (Jas. 3:5).

Like the old question 'Which comes first – the chicken or the egg?', it is hard to know whether wisdom leads to control of the tongue or controlling the tongue leads to wisdom. The book of Proverbs has much to say about the tongue. 'From the mouth of the righteous comes the fruit of wisdom, but a perverse tongue will be silenced' (Prov. 10:31). 'The words of the reckless pierce like swords, but the tongue of the wise brings healing. Truthful lips endure for ever, but a lying tongue lasts only a moment' (Prov. 12:18–19). 'The prudent keep their knowledge to themselves, but a fool's heart blurts out folly' (Prov. 12:23). 'Those who guard their mouths and their tongues keep themselves from calamity' (Prov. 21:23); '. . . a gentle tongue can break a bone' (Prov. 25:15). The Psalmist prayed, 'Set a guard over my mouth, LORD; keep watch over the door of my lips' (Ps. 141:3).

One of the most encouraging things in the book of James is at the beginning of his famous chapter – James 3 – on the tongue: 'We all stumble in many ways.' Oh yes – and the way we do it is always rooted in the inability to control what we say: 'Anyone who is never at fault in what they say is perfect, able to keep their whole body in check' (Jas. 3:2). But we are not perfect, are we? We are all going to make mistakes. None of us has perfect wisdom.

That said, James notes that the tongue is a 'small part of the body, but it makes great boasts'. He calls attention to how the slightest slip of the tongue – one unguarded comment – is like a spark that causes a forest fire. This is because the tongue is a 'spark' (Jas. 3:5–6). Whether it be pointing the finger, making a flirtatious remark that is intended to cause another to lust, making an unkind comment about someone, or saying something that does not build up a person, the consequences can be horrendous. Sometimes you never get over what was said to you. When I was ten years old I overheard that my schoolteacher said to my parents, 'R.T. is not an A student.' Until then I *was* an A student, but my grades were never good after I had heard that. It left me with an inferiority complex that I have never got over.

Your words have power – for good or ill.

James talks about two origins of wisdom – from above and from below. 'Who is wise and understanding among you? Let them show it by their good life, by deeds done in the humility that comes from wisdom' (Jas. 3:13). So how do we recognise the difference between wisdom from above and that which is from below? If there is bitterness and self-ish ambition, you can mark it down – such did not come from God. 'Such "wisdom" does not come down from heaven but is earthly, unspiritual, demonic. For where you have envy and selfish ambition, there you find disorder and every evil practice' (Jas. 3:14–16). Indeed, when the devil gets in, it 'corrupts the whole body, sets the whole course of one's life on fire, and is itself set on fire by hell' (Jas. 3:6).

This is why Paul gave another reason for practising forgiveness, namely, 'that Satan might not outwit us'; to keep us from being 'outsmarted by Satan' (2 Cor. 2:11,

NLB). What does this mean? What is the demonic when it comes to losing control of the tongue? It is when anger gets out of hand and the devil has the upper hand. He wins. Folly, not wisdom, sets in. So when I refuse to forgive – or hold a grudge – I give the devil an entry point. You can be sure that Satan will exploit our bitterness and unforgiveness to the hilt – and make fools of us.

Control of the tongue, however, brings the wisdom that comes from heaven. And how do we recognise it? It is 'first of all pure; then peace-loving, considerate, submissive, full of mercy and good fruit, impartial and sincere' (Jas. 3:17).

3 'Emergency grace'

Jesus told us that if we are called to testify before local councils, governors or kings, not to worry about 'what to say or how to say it. At that time you will be given what to say, for it will not be you speaking, but the Spirit of your Father speaking through you' (Matt. 10:19–20). I have had to call on this kind of special 'emergency grace' at least twice in my life. Once was when I was pastor of a small church in Carlisle, Ohio, in 1962–3. Some members of my church reported me to the denominational authorities for teaching false doctrine (I had said that Jesus is God). I had never had to face this sort of thing before. But my reading that very day was Matthew 10:19–20 and I knew that God would be with me. It was a wonderful experience. I had no idea what these ministers would say to me, but I was at perfect peace – the words flowed and I knew they did not come from me; instead, it was wisdom from heaven.

The second time I appealed to these verses was on 3 July 2002. I was invited by Canon Andrew White, the Archbishop of Canterbury's envoy to the Middle East, to go to Ramallah and meet President Yasser Arafat. I was actually in Israel to help lead a tour of 250 British Christians praying for peace. Andrew heard I was in Israel and asked me to meet Arafat. It was during the time the Israelis virtually destroyed all of Arafat's compound. No one was allowed in, but Andrew had unusual connections. I was able to take Lyndon Bowring and Alan Bell with me. Knowing that I was a little anxious about this, they quietly prayed for me as I was given the opportunity to speak to Arafat. The peace I had was reminiscent of what I had in Ohio in 1963. I was totally relaxed. I possibly had as much anointing on me as in any sermon I have ever preached. Dr Saeb Erekat, the chief negotiator for the Palestinians with the Israelis, sat across the table.

There is some background information you should know about. In May 1982 Arthur Blessitt and I sat in Trafalgar Square eating ice cream. I asked him about his relationship with Yasser Arafat, and he told me things that caused my heart to burn. It led me to start praying for Yasser Arafat every day. For some reason I was given a special love for him and the Palestinians. When I first met Yasser Arafat I said to him as he hugged and kissed me in Middle Eastern fashion, 'I'm your friend'. He replied, 'You're more than a friend.' I told him how I began praying for him every day twenty years earlier, and that I have possibly prayed for him more than any church leader in the world has. I told him I loved him, and tears filled his eyes. At the appropriate moment I said to him, 'The most important question, Rais [Arabic word for president], is not whether you or the Israelis get Jerusalem, but where will you be one hundred years from now?' I emphasised – at least five times – that Jesus *died* on the cross for our sins. Muslims do not believe that Jesus actually died, but that Allah delivered Jesus from the cross and took him to heaven. Arafat was quick to say, 'We believe Jesus ascended straight to heaven.' 'No, Rais,' I said, 'he died first, was raised from the dead and then went to heaven.' The visit that should have lasted fifteen minutes went to an hour and forty-five minutes. I have reported only a small portion of the dialogue. Dr Saeb Erekat also got involved, and a friendship was born between Yasser Arafat and myself. I visited him a total of five times – having lunch with him twice. On one occasion I took Mel Gibson's film on the crucifixion, *The Passion of the Christ*, into Ramallah and Arafat watched it with me along with thirty members of the Palestinian Liberation Organization (PLO). He wept as he watched it, and I prayed with him afterwards. I always prayed for him on each visit, twice anointing him with oil.

My point is this. Having been given unusual wisdom on that 3 July visit led to an amazing friendship with Arafat. The words I spoke on that first visit – and subsequent visits

– were (I believe) not my words, but words that were given to me. The big thing was that Arafat felt that I loved him. I am possibly the only American who wept when he died.

Wisdom is having the presence of the mind of the Holy Spirit. As I have said before, you will not have infallible wisdom; it is always paralleled with a blind spot, if only to keep us humble.

4 What brings PEACE

This issue is: what if you are not *sure* you have the mind of the Spirit? Is there a way to know the way forward if the immediate and direct witness of God is seemingly absent? I believe there is. I now offer an acrostic – five letters that spell PEACE – which has been a blessing to me. You need *five out of five* in order to be sure you are hearing from God. One out of five, even four out of five, is not enough. You may use this in asking for wisdom regarding guidance, the future, or when in doubt as to whether you are being led by God.

P – is it providential? Does the door open without effort or do you have to knock it down? If you have to force the door, it is not providential. When God leads through his providence he opens doors freely and clearly.

E – what would the enemy – the devil – want you to do? Most of us have a fairly shrewd idea what the devil would want us to do. Come up with that and do the opposite – and you will be pretty safe!

A – what would your supreme authority – the Bible – say? Is what you are about to do totally biblical? If there is anything in the Bible against it, drop it! Don't 'go there'. Whenever the Holy Spirit speaks you may be sure his immediate and direct word will always cohere with the Word of God.

C – does this Word – or open door – give you confidence? I find that the more I am in the will of God, the more confidence I have. If I lose confidence, something is not right.

E – does the thought of doing or saying this give you inner ease? What you feel in your 'heart of hearts' is important. The Holy Spirit will not lead you to violate your conscience. To quote Shakespeare: 'To thine own self be true.'

Do the things that make for peace (Rom. 14:17). When peace is absent this should be a glaring Red Light that says STOP. But when all five of the above come together, I believe you can be sure you are proceeding in wisdom.

There is a difference between the presence of the mind of the Spirit and the acrostic P E A C E. One is direct, the other is indirect. The acrostic P E A C E is indirect; it is *mediated* by these five points: providential, enemy, authority, confidence, ease. I offer it as a good substitute for the lack of the immediate witness of the Spirit. However, even the immediate and direct witness of the Spirit will perfectly cohere with the same acrostic! When God speaks directly and immediately you can expect doors to open, Satan to be defeated, Holy Scripture to be paramount, confidence to increase, and to have inner ease in your spirit.

10

Recognised Wisdom

Then Pharaoh said to Joseph, 'Since God has
made all this known to you, there is no one
so discerning and wise as you. You shall be in
charge of my palace, and all my people are to
submit to your orders . . .' (Gen. 41:39–40)

They will say of me, 'In the LORD alone
are deliverance and strength.' All who
have raged against him will come to him
and be put to shame. (Isa. 45:23–24)

There is possibly nothing sweeter than open vindication – when one's wisdom is recognised. So too there is possibly nothing more bitter than having to endure being misunderstood – because people questioned your wisdom. It is wonderful to have one's name cleared from a false accusation, but it is painful indeed to be looked upon with suspicion – especially by those who are regarded as wise, and by those you love.

The subject of vindication became real to me in 1956

when, following fresh insights into Scripture that went against my theological background, I was pretty much rejected by my family – my godly father, praying grandmother and other relatives, and even old friends. My dad sincerely believed I had 'broken with God' because I was now embracing a different doctrinal perspective from the way I had been taught as a child. 'Prove to me that you have not broken with God and that he is with you,' my father challenged me. I assured him that within one year from that date in August 1956 I would be totally vindicated in his eyes. A year later, however, I was not in ministry at all but working as a salesman (selling baby equipment) to pay off debts I foolishly got into. Five years later I was working as a door-to-door vacuum cleaner salesman. My father understandably felt totally justified in his doubts about me and my new theology. After all, Jesus said that wisdom is 'justified by her deeds' (Matt. 11:19, ESV; 'The proof of the pudding is in the eating', *The Message*). That said, we sometimes may be required to wait a long time for vindication – that is, external vindication.

Jesus was vindicated by the Holy Spirit (1 Tim. 3:16). This was an internal vindication; he got his joy from pleasing his Father. At his baptism there came a voice from heaven: 'This is my Son, whom I love; with him I am well pleased' (Matt. 3:17). When he was transfigured a voice from a bright cloud said, 'This is my Son, whom I love; with him I am well pleased' (Matt. 17:5). Jesus said, 'Very truly

I tell you, the Son can do nothing by himself; he can do only what he sees his Father doing' (John 5:19). 'I do not accept glory from human beings' (John 5:41). 'I always do what pleases him' (John 8:29). This vindication came by the immediate and direct witness of the Holy Spirit and was known only to Jesus. That is why it is called 'internal'. Jesus did not tell the crowds, 'I am being vindicated by the Father'. Vindication by the Spirit was Paul's observation of Jesus years later.

In a word: external vindication is when people affirm you; internal vindication is when only the Father affirms you.

Question: which would you prefer – external or internal vindication? I hope your answer is internal vindication. Here is why. People may vindicate you, but there may still be some doubt what God the Father thinks. The vindication by people may seem sweet, but what if they are wrong? Moreover, you may have the Father's vindication but not a single soul might believe in you. Could you live with that? Jesus did. He got his joy from the vindication of the Father. So should we.

But you will ask: 'Does not God want to vindicate us and reward us openly?' Yes, but there are two things that must be grasped here: (1) if we truly deserve external vindication, God will see that we get it; (2) vindication does not always come as soon as we might wish. This is why you and I must get our joy from pleasing the Father alone, and not look over our shoulders to see who agrees with us.

One reason that God delays external vindication is because time may show we don't actually deserve vindication after all! This is hard to accept. It is perhaps the hardest lesson to learn. What if, after all, you don't deserve vindication? What if you were not in the right, but in the wrong – but thought you were right and were waiting for your name to be cleared? I repeat, if you deserve to be vindicated for the stand you have taken, God will make it happen – but in his time. While we wait for external vindication we get to know God's ways. And the surprising truth is, external vindication will become less important to you. If you focus on the honour and glory of God, sooner or later external vindication will not be prized as much as internal vindication. When internal vindication means more to you than being openly vindicated, you will have achieved what God had in mind for you from the beginning.

Jesus alone is our role model. What people thought meant little or nothing to him. What the Father thought meant everything to him. Can you imagine Jesus calling one of his disciples to one side immediately after he finished the Sermon on the Mount – and asking, 'How did I do? Did I do OK? What did you think of my talk?' Hardly. He would no doubt have picked up on the fact that the people were 'amazed' at his teaching because he taught as one who had authority and not as their teachers of the law (Matt. 7:28–29). But that was not the source of his joy.

The purpose of this chapter is to persuade you to choose internal vindication – pleasing God alone. That shows a high level of wisdom. If you do that – and find total content-ment in his approval – I guarantee that external vindication will not be so important to you. The chances are that God will delay the external vindication until such time as you have shown that his approval means more than all others combined. Caution: if external vindication begins to mean too much to you, you could miss things God may want to show you. The reason the Jews missed their Messiah is because they only wanted the praise and approval of one another, and made no attempt to seek the honour and glory that comes from the only God (John 5:44).

External vindication is no doubt delightful. Who wouldn't want it? We all want it. But if it does not come in God's timing – or if you hasten to bring it on – it will be a hollow victory.

Self-vindication, then, is not on.

One more thing: vindication of wisdom is not about you or me. It is inseparably connected to *truth*. Any aspect of truth. And if it is true wisdom you are seen to have, who gave you this wisdom? 'What do you have that you did not receive?' (1 Cor. 4:7). Only God can bestow true wisdom.

If you have stood for the truth – what is clearly revealed in Scripture – you will be vindicated in God's time. In other words, vindication is not personal; it is for God's glory.

In this chapter we will see four ways that wisdom may be recognised: instantly, delayed, suspended, ultimate.

1 Instant vindication of wisdom

Sometimes God grants vindication of wisdom immediately – right on the spot. That is what happened when Solomon gave his verdict regarding who was the true mother of the living child, as we saw in Chapter 4. Instantaneously the people were in awe. Vindication of Solomon's wisdom was immediate, and he was known for his wisdom all his life. But it is not always like that. For example, young David, though anointed king and filled with the Spirit of God when Samuel poured the oil on him (1 Sam. 16:13), waited a long time before he became king. Despite behaving himself wisely in all his ways towards King Saul, he did not wear the crown for another twenty years.

At the opposite end of the spectrum, so too the fool may be recognised instantly for his or her lack of wisdom – as soon as that person opens his or her mouth. Fools show their vexation at once (Prov. 12:16); they lack the ability to demonstrate calmness in a moment of crisis or inconvenience, but always show their annoyance. And yet 'even a fool who keeps silent is considered wise; when he closes his lips he is deemed intelligent' (Prov. 17:28, ESV). A person may be esteemed as wise by nearly everyone because of his or her ability to make money. But if such people have not prepared for Eternity, they will be recognised – by God – as fools. This is what Jesus taught in the parable of the rich fool. To the person who lives only for riches in the present life, Jesus said there will be a sudden day of reckoning. It is a gross lack of wisdom to live only for the here and now and be unprepared to meet one's Maker. God will say to that person, 'You fool! This very night your life will be demanded from you' (Luke 12:20). This parable shows the possibility of an untimely death and that true wisdom will always lead one to be ready at any time to face his or her Maker. It is appointed for all people to die; after death, there is the judgment (Heb. 9:27). We must all stand before the judgment seat of Christ (2 Cor. 5:12).

Joseph

Joseph, the favourite son of Jacob, waited twenty-two years before he was vindicated before his eleven brothers, but God gave him immediate favour in a country not his own. It was with Pharaoh king of Egypt. First, Joseph showed extraordinary divine wisdom in interpreting Pharaoh's dream, but more amazing still was Joseph's prudence in voluntarily telling Pharaoh what he should do in the light of the dream. The dream indicated that Egypt would be blessed by seven years of plenty, but these would be followed by seven years of famine. Joseph advised the king to save up during the first seven years in order to have food for himself and others during the second seven years. Joseph's wisdom was immediately recognised. 'Can we find anyone like this man, one in whom is the spirit of God?' (Gen. 41:38). Pharaoh instantly made Joseph prime minister of Egypt.

Joseph might well have preferred vindication at home rather than in a foreign country, but what he wanted most he had to wait for. Sometimes God gives us honour where we least want it in order that it won't go to our heads.

The three Hebrews – Shadrach, Meshach and Abednego

These three men were forced to live in Babylon, being a part of the people of Israel that were forced to live in exile. During this time King Nebuchadnezzar demanded that all the people worship the golden image which he had built, but these three men refused to bow to it. They were singled out and severely cautioned that if they did not bow down they would be thrown alive into the burning fiery furnace. This apparently did not bother them. When they were further challenged they replied, 'Our God is able to deliver us from the burning fiery furnace but, if not, we will not bow down.' This enraged the king who had the furnace heated seven times hotter, and the three men were thrown into it. But when the king looked he said, 'I see not three but four and one is like the son of God.' These three Hebrews were prepared to be seen as fools, but their wisdom in not bowing to the golden image was instantly recognised.

Daniel

Like the previously mentioned Hebrews, Daniel was in captivity. He had been given favour by Belshazzar and became the object of jealousy by those around him who looked for a way to depose Daniel. They noticed he prayed three times a day so they made a suggestion to the king that whoever prays to 'any god or man during the next thirty days, except to you, O king, shall be thrown into the lions' den'. The king had no idea he was being manipulated and signed this decree. But Daniel's response was virtually the same as that of Shadrach, Meshach and Abednego. He continued to pray three times a day with his window wide open for all to see. The king was dismayed, but had to keep the oath and the decree he signed. Daniel was thrown into a den of lions for his disobedience. The king could not sleep. Up early the next morning, the king shouted to Daniel to see if he was still alive. Daniel replied, 'O king; live forever! My God sent his angel, and he shut the mouths of the lions.' Daniel's wisdom in defying the king's decree was instantly recognised, and the king vindicated Daniel with a new decree that all 'must reverence and fear the God of Daniel' (Dan. 6:1–27).

2 Delayed recognition of wisdom

Moses

Moses left the palace of Pharaoh at the age of forty, thinking his identification with his own people would be instantly appreciated. It wasn't, and he tried to endear himself by killing an Egyptian (Exod. 2:11–14). Not wise. Vindication for Moses' wise decision to leave the luxury of Egypt was delayed for another forty years – and more. When Moses, finally accepted by his own people, went to Pharaoh to demand the emancipation of the Israelites, he was met with horrible opposition. Not only did the king say no, but he required the Israelites to find their own straw to make the 'full quota of bricks'. The people turned on Moses (Exod. 5:22–23). It was not until after the ten plagues on Egypt, ending with the destruction of all the firstborn in Egypt, that Moses' wisdom was vindicated. But even in the wilderness, having crossed the Red Sea on dry land, the people turned on Moses yet again. They began to long for the way it had been in Egypt. Moses got his strength not from his people, but internally – from the Lord in the 'tent of meeting' where he spoke with God face to face as one talks with a friend (Exod. 33:7–11). The recognition of wisdom that is inherent in great leadership is sometimes delayed for a while – sometimes for a long time.

Jeremiah

Here is a man who was known over the centuries as 'the weeping prophet' because he knew only minimal vindication of his wisdom while he was alive. He was one of the most unappreciated prophets of all time. First, he was accused of treason because he dared to suggest that holy Jerusalem could be captured by the enemy. This to Israel was out of the question. No city on earth – ever – was as safe as Jerusalem, the place God chose to own, and with whom he would identify his name. For Jeremiah to say that the Babylonians would destroy it was not just unpatriotic; it was defying God's promise about Jerusalem. But there is more. Jeremiah was partly vindicated when Jerusalem was indeed attacked and people were taken to Babylon. But a false prophet called Hananiah stepped in to say that the captivity would only last two years. This pleased a lot of people, but Jeremiah countered that the captivity would last seventy years. This pleased nobody. Hananiah died within seven months – which was seen as a judgment upon him. The captivity in fact lasted seventy years, but Jeremiah would only be appreciated by succeeding generations. Vindication of his wisdom was delayed until after his death.

3 Suspended vindication of wisdom

One of the most enigmatic occurrences during the lifetime of the great apostle Paul was when he was warned not to go to Jerusalem by nearly everybody. But Paul was determined to go to Jerusalem during his final missionary journey. Luke, the author of Acts, was clearly on the side of those who felt Paul should *not* go to Jerusalem. Paul himself insisted he was led 'by the Spirit' to go there (Acts 20:22). But Luke later says that the disciples at Tyre 'through the Spirit' urged Paul not to go on to Jerusalem (Acts 21:4). After that, Agabus said, 'The Holy Spirit says, "In this way the Jewish leaders in Jerusalem will bind the owner of this belt and will hand him over to the Gentiles"' (Acts 21:11). Luke then says, 'When *we* heard this, *we* and the people there pleaded with Paul not to go up to Jerusalem' (Acts 21:12 – italics mine). Paul, despite his own caution not to despise prophesying (1 Thess. 5:20), replied: 'Why are you weeping and breaking my heart? I am ready not only to be bound, but also to die in Jerusalem for the name of the Lord Jesus' (Acts 21:13). When Paul would not be dissuaded, '*we* gave up and said, "The Lord's will be done"' (Acts 21:14 – italics mine). The 'we' references in the book of Acts refer to Luke himself. Whereas Acts 20:22 quotes Paul's claim that he was 'compelled by the Spirit', Luke does not agree because he states that the disciples of Tyre spoke 'through the Spirit' (Acts 21:4). Moreover, Luke is on the side of Agabus.

Who is right? Paul or these people who warned him? Most side with Paul, but I personally think Paul was wrong to defy these people. Paul's mind was made up. He went to Jerusalem, but he had little joy when he got there – virtually none (Acts 21). Paul saved his own skin when he appealed to Caesar and was allowed to go to Jerusalem (Acts 25:11–12). Paul as a man was not infallible, although he wrote with infallible inspiration in all his epistles. But Luke clearly questions Paul's wisdom as a man, despite the latter's claim to have been 'compelled by the Spirit' to go to Jerusalem.

Philippians 1:12

One of the most interesting verses in all of Paul's writings was Philippians 1:12. He writes from Rome – after the previously mentioned controversy regarding whether he should have gone to Jerusalem. The Philippians were worried about their beloved Paul. He later replies: 'Now I want you to know, brothers and sisters, that what has happened to me has actually served to advance the gospel' (Phil. 1:12). This is Paul's justification for what he did – that it served to advance the gospel. Surprise, surprise. Does this mean Paul was right to do what he did? Not necessarily. God would have overruled in any case and made sure that what Paul did served to further the gospel. This is a given! After all, even when Paul had an open door to Troas but turned it down (a very questionable decision), 'through us spreads everywhere the fragrance of the knowledge of him' (2 Cor. 2:14). Not only that, 'all things work together for good to those who love God, to those who are the called according to his purpose' (Rom. 8:28, AV). But a fundamental principle of Romans 8:28 is: *the fact that all things work together for good does not mean that what happened was right at the time.*

In a word: we have an illustration of suspended vindication here. Who was right? Was it Paul or those who warned him? You tell me!

A personal testimony

Philippians 1:12 is a very important verse for me. In April 1956 I was caught up in a painful controversy in my old church in Ashland, Kentucky. When my father wrote me a letter and instructed me to take a particular stance, it went right against all I had been led to believe. But I was shattered at the thought of going against my father; I had never done this before. Instantly I was given an immediate and direct witness of the Holy Spirit; it was as clear to me as if I had heard an audible voice: *turn to Philippians 1:12*. Never in my life had the Holy Spirit directed me to turn to a passage in the Bible without my having a clue what it said. I immediately stopped the car. I turned to Philippians 1:12 and read it in my Authorised Version of the Bible: 'But I would ye should understand, brethren, that the things which happened unto me have fallen out rather unto the furtherance of the gospel.' I knew exactly what I must do, but it meant being on the opposite side to my father in this particular controversy in Ashland. I had to make a choice between what I knew was the clear voice of the Holy Spirit and the undoubted wish of my godly father. To me, wisdom meant following the voice of the Holy Spirit. To others, wisdom would have been to listen to my dad. Nobody would have believed that I really heard the Holy Spirit. But I knew what I had to do: I obeyed the Holy Spirit. My dad disagreed; my family disagreed; my closest friends disagreed. I chose to go against everyone's wisdom. Instead of instant vindication, I found myself alone. The pain was greater than any I had ever felt, and I was outside of full-time ministry. I began working as a salesman and five years later I was selling vacuum cleaners door-to-door. This totally convinced my dear dad that I was utterly deceived. To 'fast forward' the story, years later I returned to full-time ministry; I finished my education, ending up at Oxford. I was invited to preach at Westminster Chapel and called to be the minister there in 1977 – twenty-one years after the event back in Ashland that had caused a cleavage in my relationship with my father. In 1978 – a year after I became minister of Westminster Chapel – my dad came to see and hear me. On a train from Edinburgh to King's Cross station in London, he looked at me and said, 'Son, I am proud of you. You were right and I was wrong.'

The irony is, the only 'wisdom' I had twenty-two years before was listening to what I was *absolutely sure* was the voice of the Holy Spirit. I knew that the Holy Spirit would not mislead me. To me this shows that sometimes we must stand alone and wait a good while to be vindicated.

One last anecdote in this connection. When I began a series of sermons from Philippians at Westminster Chapel in 1985, I could hardly wait to get to Philippians 1:12. God helped me on that occasion in an unprecedented manner. *In the whole of my twenty-five years at Westminster Chapel only once did I have the kind of anointing I always wanted. It was that morning.* When I finished and took my seat next to the pulpit and bowed my head, I was aware for the first time in my life of a level of anointing I had always dreamed of. It only happened once, and it was then. But two hours later one of our deacons said to me, 'I am afraid I have some disappointing news. Your sermon this morning for some reason was not recorded.' The only time I had the anointing I dreamed of was when it was not recorded. It is also the only sermon I preached in twenty-five years at the Chapel that was not recorded!

4 Ultimate recognition of wisdom

Isaiah prophesied that one day God's wisdom would be vindicated: '. . . before me every knee will bow; by me every tongue will swear. They will say of me, "In the LORD alone are deliverance and strength"' (Isa. 45:23–24). It will be on the day that God will clear his name. The prophet Habakkuk wanted to know why God allows evil when he is perfectly capable of stopping it at any moment. God promised Habakkuk an answer, but when God gave the answer it was not what Habakkuk wanted. God told Habakkuk to *wait*. The revelation – the answer to Habakkuk's prayer – would certainly come, but it would be a long time in coming (Hab. 2:1–4). The answer to the problem of evil would come in the *end* – namely, on the Final Day – when God will show himself to be a God of absolute righteousness and justice. *The whole world will see it and bow to the God of the Bible.* Not only that; 'at the name of Jesus every knee should bow, in heaven and on earth and under the earth, and every tongue acknowledge that Jesus Christ is Lord, to the glory of God the Father' (Phil. 2:10–11).

At long last there will be universally recognised wisdom – when God clears his name. No greater external vindication than this is possible. In the meantime, let us obtain our vindication internally – the way Jesus got his.

11

The Fool

Fools despise wisdom and instruction. (Prov. 1:7)

But God said to him, 'You fool! This very
night your life will be demanded from
you . . . This is how it will be with whoever
stores up things for themselves but is not
rich towards God.' (Luke 12:20–21)

Just as there can be instant recognition of wisdom, so also – at the opposite end of the spectrum – there is often instant recognition of the fool. The book of Proverbs repeatedly contrasts the wise man with the fool because the polar opposite of the wise man is the fool. 'Fools show their annoyance at once' (Prov. 12:16), whereas the wise man holds his tongue and demonstrates patience; it is 'to one's glory to overlook an offence' (Prov. 19:11). This coheres with James's description of wisdom that comes from heaven – peace-loving and gentle. Wisdom that is earthly and of the devil is what you expect from a fool – jealousy and disorder (Jas. 3:15–18).

And yet it can take years for a fool to look in a mirror and see what has long been so obvious to others. At the end of his tragic life King Saul stated, 'I have played the fool' (1 Sam. 26:21; AV – 'I have acted like a fool and have erred greatly'; ESV – 'I have acted foolishly and have made a great mistake'). This folly was apparent for approximately twenty years, but Saul had no objectivity about himself. It was truly evident early on in his kingship when he unthinkably put his distressed and weakened soldiers under an oath, saying, 'Cursed be anyone who eats food before evening comes, before I have avenged myself on my enemies!' (1 Sam. 14:24). Nothing could be worse for fighting men who needed strength, nourishment and energy from food. King Saul was even lacking common sense. That is almost always the case with the fool; they forfeit common sense.

When did this folly first emerge in Saul? He had such a good beginning. He was given another heart (1 Sam. 10:9), a prophetic gift (1 Sam. 10:10), and had such authority in the early days of his kingship that 'the terror of the LORD fell on the people' (1 Sam. 11:7). But at some stage he began to take himself too seriously. He was told to wait for Samuel to offer the burnt offerings, a religious ritual according to the Mosaic Law. But Samuel was held up and Saul became impatient, claiming he was 'compelled' to offer the burnt offering (1 Sam. 13:12). His salient absence of sound judgment was evident when he wilfully and consciously transgressed the Ceremonial Law. The Law made it clear that only the person called of God could participate in the offerings (Num. 16:40; Exod. 30:7–9). Saul took upon himself offering the burnt offerings (1 Sam. 13:9). At some point during this time the wisdom and authority that had been present in Saul began to lift. He was left to himself and demonstrated gross folly and utter absence of wisdom from then on; and never got the previously mentioned authority back again.

Whatever possessed Saul to break the Ceremonial Law? That in itself was folly. You have two things happening here: King Saul's *command* – 'Bring me the burnt offering', and the *deed* – when he actually 'offered up the burnt offering' (1 Sam. 13:9). Between the command and the deed Saul might have stopped himself. Perhaps someone should have said, 'Your majesty, sir, you should not be doing that.' But they would have been too afraid to counsel the king. In any case, Saul would have no doubt replied, 'I am king, therefore I can do anything.'

My point is, Saul's very command for them to bring the burnt offerings showed his lack of wisdom; but after he carried out the task his folly descended to an even lower point and was compounded. He got nothing right after that for the rest of his tragic life.

Sin always has at least two basic ingredients: (1) temptation, and (2) giving into it. It is not a sin to be tempted. When Saul claimed that he felt 'compelled' to offer the burnt offerings this was the onset of temptation, but he also gave in to this temptation. It was tantamount to passing the buck to God – as if either God was responsible for what he felt or

God had told him to do it. There are people who claim to have heard from God when such a 'word' goes right against Scripture! It is some people's way of justifying their foolish decision by implying that God was behind their deeds. A sure way to become yesterday's man or woman is to assert that God has told you something that in fact defies Holy Scripture. That was almost certainly the pivotal point in Saul's life that resulted in his total downfall.

And yet there is something in all of us that makes us want to blame God for things we know we should not have done. James warns us that, 'When tempted, no one should say, "God is tempting me." For God cannot be tempted by evil, nor does he tempt anyone; but each person is tempted when they are dragged away by their own evil desire and enticed. Then, after desire has conceived, it gives birth to sin; and sin, when it is full-grown, gives birth to death' (Jas. 1:13–15). Saul lived another twenty years, but his suicidal finish is a demonstration of one who took himself too seriously, was motivated by fear and jealousy, was not accountable to Samuel as he should have been, and who flagrantly went against the Word of God.

Etymology

There are two Greek words that are translated 'fool' in the New Testament. One is the Greek *moros* from which we get the word 'moron'. Used thirteen times in the New

Testament, this Greek word in ancient times was applied to someone who was stupid or unintelligent. One would surely not call a person a moron if he or she could not help it that they were not too bright? We vent our anger by calling people names like 'moron', 'imbecile' or 'idiot'. In other words, one of the most cutting ways of putting an intelligent person down is to imply that he or she is unintelligent. Jesus said if you call a person a fool – as in moron or idiot – you are in danger of the fire of hell (Matt. 5:22). The other word is *aphron* – which means the opposite of *phren*, which means 'mind' or 'understanding'; therefore *aphron* means 'imprudent' or 'foolish'. It is used twelve times in the New Testament. Both Greek words point to one's mental faculty, implying that a person is empty-headed. But *aphron* is also used also to denote 'ungodliness'.

In Robert McLaughlin's commentary on Ecclesiastes, he lists five categories of fools. First, the *stupid* fool (Hebrew, *pethiy*), one easily persuaded by flattery or delusion. This person is ready to believe almost anything and exhibits great gullibility. He believes in gossip, slander, false teaching and hates academic discipline (Prov. 1:22; 14:15; 22:3). Second, the *unreasonable* fool (Hebrew, *ewil*). The word means to be perverse. This person despises wisdom and instruction. He is full of talk, and the only way he can appear wise is to keep his mouth shut (Prov. 1:7; 12:15; 14:3; 17:28; 20:3). Third, the *stubborn* fool (Hebrew, *kesil*). He is dull and passive, and has trouble coping with authority in business or with spiritual leaders. He boasts to other people of his own ability. He is two-faced, hypocritical and loves to slander (Prov. 1:22; 10:18; 13:20; 14:7, 16; 15:14; 17:10, 12; 18:2). Fourth, the *scorning or mocking* fool (Hebrew, *latsats*). He is stupid, wicked, vile. He is flirting with a reprobate mind, and will even scoff at Holy Scripture. He is blind and deaf to spiritual matters (Prov. 1:22; 9:7–8; 13:1; 14:6; 22:10). Fifth, there is the *committed* fool (Hebrew, *nabal*). He may well have entered apostasy (Ps. 14:1; Job 2:10; Ezek. 13:3; 17:21). Abigail said to David, 'Please pay no attention, my lord, to that wicked man Nabal. He is just like his name – his name means fool, and folly goes with him' (1 Sam. 25:25).

Perhaps the greatest malady of a fool is that he or she seldom – if ever – admits to being wrong.

The 'fool' in the Bible – whatever the Hebrew or Greek word – is not given this title as an insult, nor is the word used in angry exaggeration. The designation 'fool' in the Bible is never imputed to a person with a *natural* lack of intelligence, something that he or she cannot help. The fool in the Bible *chose* to be a fool. Partly what makes a fool a *fool* is that this person is in fact intelligent. Being a fool is an act of the will. When you see the word 'fool' in the Bible it describes a person who wilfully but unnecessarily made imprudent choices. It is *not* the result of an unavoidable congenital condition. Whether the 'fool' is in the book of Proverbs or in the New Testament, he or she is a person who is stupid or dull – but it is *always* that person's own fault. The fool has made his or her own bed; foolishness is a choice. The fool 'did not *choose* to fear the LORD' (Prov. 1:29 – my italics).

The use of the word 'fool' in the Bible, then, is not given in anger, aimed to embarrass someone, or to insult. It is merely a description of the sad condition of one who chose not to fear the Lord. 'The mouths of fools are their undoing, and their lips are a snare to their very lives' (Prov. 18:7). 'As a dog returns to its vomit, so fools repeat their folly' (Prov. 26:11). 'Why should fools have money in hand to buy wisdom, when they are not able to understand it?' (Prov. 17:16); '. . . a fool is hotheaded and yet feels secure' (Prov. 14:16); '. . . every fool is quick to quarrel' (Prov. 20:3). This is why it is said that 'even a fool is thought wise if he keeps silent' (Prov. 17:28). The problem is, such a fool normally cannot keep quiet! 'All who are prudent act with knowledge, but fools expose their folly' (Prov. 13:16). 'The way of fools seems right to them, but the wise listen to advice' (Prov. 12:15). Whereas keeping God's commands 'will keep you from the adulterous woman' (Prov. 7:5), the fool lets the adulteress lead him astray, 'little knowing it will cost him his life' (Prov. 7:23).

Once a fool, always a fool?

I will admit, however, that one of the uneasy feelings I get when reading the book of Proverbs is that these conditions seem permanent. Yet they are not meant to be grasped in that way. They describe *possibilities* – whatever the Greek or Hebrew word – and do not imply that you are unconditionally locked in to be one or the other. Also, one's natural temperament does not seem to be taken into account in the book of Proverbs. I have a phlegmatic friend who seems always as cool as a cucumber – even if running late for a train or plane – whereas I would be a nervous wreck. You therefore might get the impression from Proverbs that your unchangeable lot is either to be a wise person *or* a fool. If so, I have to come clean right now and say that many depictions of a fool describe me at times and point to my own foolishness. 'Fools show their annoyance at once' (Prov. 12:16). Oh dear – that's me. 'Do you see someone who speaks in haste? There is more hope for a fool than for them' (Prov. 29:20). If speaking in haste renders one to be a fool, I think I must be the greatest fool that ever was. I have shown myself to be foolish too many times – in private and even in the pulpit. Even the words 'the way of fools seems right to them' (Prov. 12:15) give me pause for thought – I often think I am right. But it is always a timely word that should make me double-check my opinions.

The fool therefore – whatever the Hebrew words that show different kinds of fool – is not locked into being foolish for ever. The fool is not in an irrevocable, irretrievable and hopeless condition. There is hope for the fool. This is why the psalmist asked, '. . . you fools, when will you become wise?' (Ps. 94:8). Paul exhorted, 'Wake up, sleeper, rise from the dead, and Christ will shine on you' (Eph. 5:14).

We have all been fools at one time or another. Thank God that we don't have to *remain* fools. Thank God that a foolish moment does not mean we are in that state for ever. A fool is a person who cannot control his tongue. And yet 'we all stumble in many ways,' says James. I am so glad he said that. 'Anyone who is never at fault in what they say is perfect, able to keep their whole body in check' (Jas. 3:2). I have ignited more than one forest fire with my impertinent comments in my lifetime, as James put it (Jas. 3:5). And even in our wisest and most mature state we are capable of lapsing into folly by the unguarded comment, hasty judgment, being defensive when criticised or taking ourselves too seriously. Here are words to ponder: 'Do you see a person wise in their own eyes? There is more hope for a fool than for them' (Prov. 26:12). This is a caution – suggested twice by the apostle Paul (Rom. 11:25; Rom. 12:16) – that will bear our constant examination. I know what it is to have preached a sermon that (I thought) was about as good as they get. I can say to myself, 'At last I have learned how to preach.' And God looks down at me lovingly and says, 'Really?', because the next time I try to preach I make a complete mess of it. This scenario has happened to me more times than I care to think about.

Two parables

Jesus said in the parable of the ten virgins that in the final generation just before his Second Coming the Church would be depicted as ten virgins: five of them wise and five of them foolish. All, however, are asleep. The wise are those Christians who are pursuing their inheritance – by taking oil in their lamps as they wait for the bridegroom. The foolish are those who do not pursue their inheritance – taking no oil with them. In the middle of the night the whole Church is awakened and the foolish realise they should have seen this coming. They say to the wise, 'Give us some of your oil; our lamps are going out' (Matt. 25:7). But the wise virgins have barely enough for themselves (Matt. 25:1–6). One of the things that stand out in this parable is that their being awakened did not change anyone's spiritual state; it merely exposed what their conditions were. The foolish did not become wise. It was too late.

Please note: that situation – when it is too late to change – sadly will be the case when this Great Awakening takes place. But it need not be the case with you and me *now*. God gives warnings because we can do something about our spiritual condition. We don't have to remain foolish. This is why I have written this book.

Jesus gave another parable in which he invokes the word 'fool'. In the parable of the rich fool he described a rich man who decided to make more money than ever. This man said to himself, 'You have plenty of good things laid up for many years. Take life easy; eat, drink, and be merry.'

Could that describe you? Have you assumed you have plenty of time left? Have you said, 'One day I will sort things out and become what I know I should be'? There is one more verse I will quote from the book of Proverbs:

'Whoever remains stiff-necked after many rebukes will suddenly be destroyed – without remedy' (Prov. 29:1).

In Jesus' parable in which the rich man said he had many years left, God unexpectedly said to him, 'You fool! This very night your life will be demanded from you.' There was no more notice given, no more warning. Jesus added a P.S.: 'This is how it will be with whoever stores up things for themselves but is not rich towards God' (Luke 12:20–21).

Once a fool, always a fool? No. But don't let it happen to you.

12

The Wisdom of Jesus

And Jesus grew in wisdom and stature, and
in favour with God and man. (Luke 2:52)

'If then David calls him "Lord", how can he
be his son?' No one could say a word in reply,
and from that day on no one dared to ask
him any more questions. (Matt. 22:45–46)

The wisest man who ever lived was Jesus of Nazareth. He is the only person in human history who perfectly fulfilled the Law and never sinned. He is the only man who never put a foot wrong – in thought, word or deed. Jesus had perfect wisdom. 'We all stumble in many ways,' said James; indeed if we are never at fault in what we *say* we are 'perfect' (Jas. 3:2). And that is precisely what Jesus was – perfect. No deceit was found in his mouth (1 Pet. 2:20). He was tempted just like we are, but in his case it was without sin (Heb. 4:15).

The two wisest men in the Old Testament were Moses and Solomon, and, as we have seen, neither of these was perfect. Moses excelled in leadership and theological wisdom. Solomon excelled in practical wisdom; the books of Proverbs and Ecclesiastes are said to have been written by him. Both Moses and Solomon are compared to Jesus in the New Testament. 'For the Law was given through Moses; grace and truth came through Jesus Christ' (John 1:17). Solomon was famous for his wisdom. The queen of the South came from the 'ends of the earth' to hear his wisdom, yet Jesus was 'greater than Solomon' (Luke 11:31). Jesus exceeded Moses in theological wisdom and leadership skills; he surpassed Solomon in every kind of wisdom.

All the definitions of wisdom I gave in Chapter 1 perfectly describe Jesus' wisdom – whether it be his teaching, his relationship with the Father, or in his human relationships. Whether wisdom is knowing the Father's opinion, the ability to get things done, having 20/20 foresight vision, knowing the next step forward, what to do and say (and when to say it), or having the presence of the mind of the Holy Spirit, Jesus' wisdom was demonstrated to utter perfection. Whereas you and I have the Holy Spirit in 'measure' (Rom. 12:3), Jesus had the Holy Spirit 'without limit' (John 3:34).

Developed wisdom

I have been fascinated that the wisdom of Jesus is mentioned not only with reference to his teaching, but also his miracles. When he taught in the synagogue 'many who heard him were amazed'. Then they asked, 'What's this wisdom that has been given to him, that he even does miracles!' (Mark 6:2–3). The implication is that it was in some sense his wisdom that was connected to the miracles. Could it be that God would extend the power for us to do the miraculous if we made wisdom a priority?

And yet Jesus' wisdom was being developed – from childhood right up to his death on the cross. This is extraordinary, and it may surprise you. Keep in mind we are looking at Jesus the man. He was the eternal God made flesh (John 1:14). He was God as though he were not man; he was man as though he were not God. He was the God-man. Truly God, but truly *man*. One of the earliest heresies in Christology had to do with denying Jesus' humanity. It seems the early Church embraced his deity far more quickly than they did his humanity. The Apostles' Creed was almost certainly written largely to affirm Jesus as a *man*. Docetism (from the Greek word *dokeo* – to appear) was the ancient heresy that Jesus only 'appeared' to be a man, but he was not truly a man. The funny thing is, some Christians today are in more danger of accepting a docetic Christology – that Jesus is God but only seems to be a man – than affirming that he was and is totally a man. There are a surprising number of evangelical Christians who are afraid to say much about Jesus being truly man lest they border on denying his deity. But it is just as heretical to deny Jesus' humanity as to deny that he is God.

In Chapter 10 we saw that Jesus should be our role model. In this final chapter we need to see exactly what I mean by that – and why the wisdom of Jesus should be our aim. Keep in mind that we are looking only at his humanity in this chapter. He lived on this planet for thirty-three years as a human being. During his lifetime he was never vindicated by people, but only vindicated by the Holy Spirit (1 Tim. 3:16). You will recall that this was an internal vindication – the approval of the Father.

Jesus as a child developed in wisdom. There are many verses in the Bible I don't understand, and one of them is how he 'grew in wisdom and stature, and in favour with God and man' (Luke 2:52). Does this mean he was a child prodigy? He had the Holy Spirit without limit (John 3:34), but was he given the Spirit without limit from his birth? Or at his conception? He was truly God and truly man from conception, yes. But was he filled with the Holy Spirit when the Word became flesh in the womb of the Virgin Mary – or did having the Spirit without limit come at his bar mitzvah at the age of twelve? He spoke about doing his Father's business at that time. How could he dazzle the rabbinic authorities when he was only twelve years old? People were 'amazed at his understanding and his answers' (Luke 2:47). Or did he receive the Holy Spirit without limit at his baptism when he was about thirty years of age? Even more baffling to me is how the Son of God – who had the Holy Spirit without limit – would learn obedience by *suffering* (Heb. 5:19)?

Jesus developed physically and spiritually as any child would do. He would need correction from his parents.

Would he ever need a spanking? You tell me. He would need to learn. Would he have to read something twice to understand it? You tell me. He certainly learned to read and write in Hebrew or Aramaic and do his multiplication tables (if they did maths in those days). He would read the Bible – the Old Testament: the Law, the prophets, the historical books, the Psalms and Proverbs. You can safely presume that he not only read his Old Testament, but knew it backwards and forwards. At what age? Who knows? It is my own view that when the Holy Spirit came down like a dove at his baptism by John the Baptist, he *fully* grasped that he was the Son of God. That is when his messianic consciousness set in; that is when he fully knew his mission.

But he developed in wisdom right to the end – that is, to his death. Why? Did not having the Spirit without limit take care of any deficiency in wisdom? Why did he have to develop in wisdom after receiving the Spirit without limit? Answer: it is because he needed to learn how to *sympathise with us*. Part of his role as Redeemer was that he would be our high priest. The high priest in the Old Testament would 'deal gently with those who are ignorant and are going astray' (Heb. 5:2), but he did not know how to be empathetic; he was mainly concerned with the intricacies of the liturgy of the Ceremonial Law. But Jesus our high priest was different. In order to be our merciful and faithful high priest 'he had to be made like them, fully human in every way' (Heb. 2:17). Therefore because 'he himself suffered when he was tempted, he is able to help those who are being

215

tempted' (Heb. 2:18). This is why he is touched with the feeling of our weaknesses (Heb. 4:15, AV).

But there is more. One of the most difficult verses in the Bible to me is this: although Jesus was the Son of God, 'he learned obedience from what he suffered'. That is not all; this obedience is what perfected him as our great high priest. It is not what made him sinless. He would have been sinless in any case. But once he was 'made perfect' in the sense of having wisdom and compassion to sympathise with us, 'he became the source of eternal salvation' (Heb. 5:9). He who 'knew no sin was made sin' (2 Cor. 5:21, AV) on the cross that we might become the righteousness of God in him.

A theological question is, could Jesus have been our Saviour had he died as a child or teenager? The answer is, probably not. Because part of being our substitute was that he had to go through what you and I have to go through. He not only took our place on the cross; he was our substitute throughout the whole of his life. As a man he had perfect faith and fulfilled the Law – perfectly. Although he would have been the God-man had he died as an infant or teenager, he would not have known the entire gamut of suffering until he went through every conceivable trial and temptation you and I face. He was tempted in 'every way' (Heb. 4:15). And when I say his suffering went on *right to the end*, meaning the cross, never forget that his most severe temptation and trial was during the last twenty-four hours of his life.

For example, he suffered utter loneliness in Gethsemane. He took his inner circle – Peter, James and John – into this garden. While he prayed, they slept. He asked why they could not be there for him for a mere hour? But they still slept. When he became resigned to the horrible fact of utter loneliness – that he was not going to have their companionship and sympathy to the very end – he said to them, 'Sleep on now' (Matt. 26:45, AV). When the writer of Hebrews refers to his offering up 'prayers and petitions with fervent cries and tears' (Heb. 5:7), it was almost certainly a reference to Gethsemane. All this was so he could be the Perfect Substitute for us – both by a sinless life and sacrificial death, but also so that he would be able to sympathise, having gone through it himself. The wonder is, though Jesus is now free from pain, he never forgot what it was like to be tempted and tested during the days of his earthly sojourn. He is 'touched' with the feeling of our weaknesses (Heb. 4:15, AV). Hallelujah, what a Saviour!

When I say Jesus is our role model, we must never forget that if the Son of God needed to learn obedience through suffering, how much more you and me? Do you pray for wisdom? Then expect suffering to accompany this pursuit. 'For with much wisdom comes much sorrow; the more knowledge, the more grief' (Eccles. 1:18). Suffering is the way Jesus was perfected in wisdom to be our great high priest. Do you want to be perfected in wisdom in order that you might be used of the Lord? Then I have to tell you that there are no short-cuts in this pursuit.

There are at least two ways of coming into a greater anointing of the Holy Spirit. One is by the ever-increasing measure of the Spirit being imparted to us. The other is through suffering. Speaking personally, I have had almost every high-profile Christian under the sun to pray for me or lay hands on me – from Martyn Lloyd-Jones to Rodney Howard-Browne (and hundreds in between). Although I never felt anything consciously at the time when I was being prayed for, I never underestimate what the laying on of hands can do to increase one's anointing. But if I am totally candid, I suspect that whatever ability I may have to understand and teach the Bible has come mostly through disappointment, betrayal, suffering, forgiving and praying for my enemies. If Jesus had to do this, so do I. And so do you if you aspire to Jesus' wisdom.

Christ's wisdom, then, was always developing and maturing. Even on the cross Jesus was tested to the hilt. Had he once – even once – retorted in anger or self-pity when he was being mocked, the entire plan of redemption would have been called off. But Jesus never sinned. The words 'It is finished' (the Greek word *tetelestai*) just before he died (John 19:30) not only meant 'paid in full', but also marked the moment his suffering was finally over. 'It ain't over til it's over', as Yogi Berra, the famous baseball catcher for the New York Yankees, used to say. For Jesus the suffering wasn't over until the very end. But when he breathed his last breath, the suffering was *over*. So too with you and me. We must resist the temptation to get vengeance and give in to self-pity right to the end if we want to finish well. We won't do it perfectly, but Jesus is the only model for this. Aim for his developed and perfected wisdom.

Directed wisdom

We now look at the key to his perfect wisdom. Jesus was not his 'own man'. He himself said so: '. . . the Son can do nothing by himself; he can do only what he sees his Father doing, because whatever the Father does the Son also does' (John 5:19). There is perfect unity in the God-head. The Son never ran ahead of the Father, never said anything the Father did not direct him to say, nor did he heal anybody unless it originated with the Father. Jesus said that the Holy Spirit had the exact same relationship with the Father that he had. The Holy Spirit 'will not speak on his own; he will speak only what he hears' (John 16:13). The Authorised Version (sadly) mistranslated John 16:13, saying that the Spirit would not speak of himself – which not only misses the point, but is misleading. A lot of sincere Christians have been hesitant to talk about the Holy Spirit since the Authorised Version says the Holy Spirit doesn't talk about himself. That is not the meaning at all. The meaning is this: as Jesus could do nothing by himself but only what was directed by the Father, so too the Holy Spirit would not speak on his own, but do or say only what was directed by the Father. There is perfect unity in the Trinity.

What is the point? Our heavenly Father directs both the Son and the Spirit in what to say and do. The reason, then, that Jesus had perfect wisdom is that he took his cue from the Father and never ran ahead of him. The Son's actions and words mirrored those of the Father. As the Father had perfect wisdom, so too the Son. And as Jesus has perfect wisdom, so also the Holy Spirit. To the degree you and I have the presence of the mind of the Holy Spirit, we will know we are proceeding in true wisdom.

Therefore when you read the four Gospels – whether it be Jesus' teachings, his miracles, or disputations with the Pharisees – keep in mind that Jesus was perfectly carrying out the Father's direction. This meant that Jesus' enemies were really up against God the Father – not merely Jesus. The Father was telling Jesus what to say.

Why is this important? First, to see the humility of Jesus. He never claimed greatness for himself; he was utterly unpretentious. He got his joy not from the compliments of the people, but solely from knowing he pleased the Father. That is another dimension of what is meant by vindication by the Spirit (1 Tim. 3:16). It was the immediate and direct witness of the Spirit from the Father that gave Jesus his contentment and satisfaction. Second, this teaching is vital for you and me if we want to pursue his wisdom – that is, the wisdom of Jesus. But with a difference. You and I do not have the Holy Spirit without limit; only Jesus has that. Moreover, Jesus never grieved the Holy Spirit. That is why the Dove came down on Jesus and 'remained' (John

1:32–33). The Holy Spirit *stayed* on Jesus when he came down. With you and me (I'm afraid) the Dove comes down, but flies away when we grieve him by an unguarded comment, bitterness or unforgiveness (Eph. 4:30–32). This is a metaphor of course; for the Holy Spirit never really leaves us. But when we grieve the Spirit we lose that intimacy that enables us to hear clearly from the Father. Jesus never lost that. His wisdom therefore came directly from the Father without the slightest variance between what the Father directed and what Jesus did.

One of the more haunting lines in Proverbs is 'Sin is not ended by multiplying words, but the prudent hold their tongues' (Prov. 10:19). I have often found – to my embarrassment – this to be so true. When a conversation is lengthy, chances are you will say something that is unguarded, unfortunate, unkind or unhelp-ful. But because Jesus only spoke what the Father ordered, he could talk all day long – whether teaching publicly or speaking with a group of enemies – and never sin.

You and I may truly have the immediate and direct witness of the Spirit. We too may experience vindication by the Spirit – seeking the approval of the Father and not from people. But always remember that at best the Holy Spirit is given in measure with us, not an unlimited measure as it was with Jesus. What we must do, then, is to avoid grieving the Holy Spirit by the slightest holding of a grudge or speaking evil of someone. The Holy Spirit will not bend the rules for any of us. If we learn what grieves the Spirit – and not do that – we will get closer and closer to the wisdom that Jesus demonstrated on earth. Jesus listened to the Father; he did not run ahead or behind the will of the Father. Jesus never spoke on his own; he waited for the Father to direct him.

Jesus never sought his own glory. We too must never seek our own glory – ever. We therefore must be in consistent and constant pursuit of *his* wisdom. To the degree that we may approximate that wisdom, we must be extremely careful to give God the glory – as Jesus did. The moment we begin to be wise in our own eyes we border on becoming the fool as described in the book of Proverbs. You may recall that there is more hope for a fool than for one who is wise in his own eyes (Prov. 26:12).

Mary and Martha

Mary and Martha in the New Testament provide an example of directed wisdom. They were sisters who lived in a village called Bethany, very near Jerusalem. Martha invited Jesus to have a meal with them. Martha did all the work, and Mary spent the whole time sitting at Jesus' feet listening to all he had to say. Martha was preoccupied with getting the meal ready; but instead of asking Mary to help her, she turned on Jesus and asked: 'Lord, don't you care that my sister left me to do the work by myself? Tell her to help me!'

Jesus' reply to Martha was a rather surprising word, and yet one that none of us should ever forget: '"Martha, Martha," the Lord answered, "you are worried and upset about many things, but few things are needed – or indeed only one. Mary has chosen what is better, and it will not be taken away from her"' (Luke 10:41–42). Jesus' wisdom affirmed Mary's wisdom – to spend time directly in the presence of Jesus. According to him, Mary chose what is *necessary*. He did not rebuke Martha harshly – he merely described what she was feeling. But Mary's wisdom prevailed on that occasion. One can always eat a meal – but it is soon gone. Time with Jesus lasts for ever.

When I first met Russian Christians years ago, one of them astutely described what he perceived as the difference between Western and Eastern Christianity: 'You people are more like Martha,' the pastor of the Moscow Baptist Church lovingly said to me, 'we are more like Mary.'

Demonstrated wisdom

I have had to be selective in referring to the many displays of Jesus' wisdom. *All* Jesus ever said or did was carried out with perfect wisdom – from how he was led to when he died, from how and when he healed, to how he put the Pharisees in their place.

Theological wisdom

Jesus was and is the greatest theologian that ever lived. Jesus is primarily thought of as a great teacher, and we tend to think of Paul as being the great theologian. But Paul was in fact the greatest *interpreter* of Jesus; he was actually *taught directly* by Jesus. Jesus was not only the wisest person who ever lived, but also the greatest theologian of all time. Paul got his teaching not from man, but 'by revelation *from* Jesus Christ' (Gal. 1:12 – my italics). When Paul spoke of what he received by the 'word of the Lord' – whether referring to practical living (1 Cor. 7:10) or eschatology (1 Thess. 4:15) – you could say that Paul was being spoon-fed by Jesus. This is why Paul is the main writer of the New Testament to unveil the teachings of Jesus and to explain why Jesus died.

Jesus most perfectly understood the Mosaic Law and was the first to know why it needed to be fulfilled to the hilt if anybody was to get to heaven. Near the beginning of his ministry Jesus promised to *fulfil the Law* (Matt. 5:17), which was 'the most stupendous statement' Jesus ever made, said Dr Martyn Lloyd-Jones. As I said above, Jesus knew his Old Testament backwards and forwards. He also knew that no human being had ever kept the Mosaic Law. He equally realised the extraordinary implications of what he said when he stated that he himself *would* fulfil it. This meant that sixty seconds a minute, sixty minutes an hour, and twenty-four hours a day, every day of his life Jesus would live without one sin. Amazing.

Jesus therefore knew why he alone must fulfil the Law. First, the Law demanded fulfilment. Second, no person had ever fulfilled it. Third, he alone could do it, and that is why he promised that he would do it. Therefore by doing and saying only what the Father directed him to say and do, he would would carry out the demands of the Law – every jot and tittle of it. This meant keeping over 2,000 pieces of Mosaic legislation. He knew his Father to be essentially a God of justice and mercy. Justice means that God must punish us because we are sinners. Mercy means that God does not want to punish us. There was one way, however, that God could be just and merciful at the same time. That was if Jesus himself kept the Law, including fulfilling the sacrificial system. He knew he would have to die as a sacrifice, like a lamb. He also knew that if he sinned at any time in his entire life, he would fail in his mission. All that Jesus did on this earth was for us. If he sinned at any time – even once – he would not be the perfect substitute. Therefore by a sinless life and a sacrificial death the Mosaic Law would be fulfilled. God's wrath would be perfectly and totally satisfied – so he could be merciful to us. Jesus was not trying to impress the Jews with his infallible theological knowledge, but he had complete knowledge and knew what had to be done. It was mainly the apostle Paul who interpreted all this in his writings. But had Jesus not *known* what was required of him, then Paul would have had nothing to say concerning how we are saved.

Jesus' practical theology

By this I mean, how then shall we live? Jesus' teachings show us what is required for us to *inherit* the kingdom of heaven, and all of us are called to come into our inheritance. Some do; some don't. The Sermon on the Mount is chiefly about the kingdom of heaven and the requirement to enter it, namely: (1) by trusting Jesus' righteousness since he was our substitute – having fulfilled the Law for us, and (2) by our 'exceeding' the righteousness of the Pharisees (Matt. 5:20). I go into this in detail in my book called *The Sermon on the Mount*. The Pharisees only conceived of the external righteousness of the Law being kept – as, for example, not committing the act of murder or adultery. But exceeding the righteousness of the Pharisees meant not hating or lusting – an internal righteousness (Matt. 5:21–30). This is the way one *inherits* the kingdom. This is what Jesus taught the apostle Paul and what Paul has taught us.

Appealing to our self-interest

I mentioned this above. It should not surprise us that Jesus upheld a tradition that goes back to Abraham – appealing to one's self-interest to get someone's attention. God told Abraham to leave home and go to another land and that his name would be 'great' (Gen. 12:1–2). Moses left the palace of Pharaoh because of the 'reward' (Heb. 11:26). God told people to tithe and therefore be blessed so much they would not have room enough for it (Mal. 3:10). Jesus said if you are persecuted for Christ then your reward in heaven would be 'great' (Matt. 5:12). Do you like to be judged? 'Do not judge, and you will not be judged' (Luke 6:37). If someone says to you, 'I don't serve the Lord for reward, I do it only for his glory', they are either emitting thinly disguised self-righteousness or are bubbling over with pseudo-humility. God has *always* motivated people through an entry point of their self-interest. This is his wisdom. It was the wisdom of Jesus.

Messianic consciousness

Jesus knew that the Son in Psalm 110 referred to himself: 'The LORD says to my lord: "Sit at my right hand until I make your enemies a footstool for your feet"' (Ps. 110:1). So he put a question to the Pharisees: 'What do you think about the Christ? Whose son is he?' They replied: 'The son of David.' Then Jesus asked them, 'How is it then that David, speaking by the Spirit, calls him "Lord"?' He concluded: 'If then David calls him "Lord", how can he be his son?' No one could reply; '. . . from that day on no one dared to ask him any more questions' (Matt. 22:41–46). They had been confronted with divine wisdom by an infallible theologian – the Son of God.

By the way, in this conversation there is contained Jesus' own doctrine of Holy Scripture. David the psalmist spoke 'by the Spirit', said Jesus (Matt. 22:43). The New Testament doctrine of inspiration states that all Scripture is God-breathed and written by the guidance of the Holy Spirit (2 Tim. 3:16; 2 Pet. 2:21).

The kingdom

Jesus knew that his own disciples – despite his continued teaching – thought that the kingdom of God referred to an earthly empire (Acts 1:6). He made it as clear as he could that the kingdom came not with observation, but is within us (Luke 17:20–21). Jesus gave a parable which, if they could understand it, showed that their idea of the kingdom was wrong (Luke 19:11–26). He did not try to correct them, but let them wait until after the Holy Spirit fell on them at Pentecost. This too was part of his wisdom. He said that he had many things he could say to them but that they were not able to bear them now (John 16:12). Had he taught them what they could not bear, it would have been tantamount to casting pearls before pigs – which he warned against (Matt. 7:6). We are all like pigs at one time or another. We may fancy that we are able to receive 'all there is' – not unlike the disciples' thinking (Matt. 20:22) – but our Lord wisely and graciously leads us not directly from A to Z, but one step at a time: from A to B.

Life beyond the grave

Jesus knew the true and ultimate meaning of the phrase 'God of Abraham, Isaac and Jacob' in Exodus 3:6, although the Sadducees fancied themselves to be the true experts on that verse. Jesus showed that the reference to Abraham, Isaac and Jacob in Exodus 3:6 did not merely prove that these three patriarchs were at the beginning of Israel's historical roots, but were still *alive and well* – a word that astonished everyone. The Sadducees thought that the words of Exodus 3:6 ('I am the God of Abraham, the God of Isaac and the God of Jacob') meant only that these ancient historical figures had once lived and were *chosen* by God; they did not believe they could possibly still be alive. It did not cross the minds of the Sadducees that Exodus 3:6 in fact meant Abraham, Isaac and Jacob were literally *alive and conscious at that moment* – a teaching that went right against that of those who did not believe in any sort of life beyond the grave. Indeed, Jesus told them that God is not the God of the dead, but of the 'living' (Matt. 22:23–33). His wisdom 'silenced the Sadducees' (Matt. 22:34).

Understanding of the human heart

Jesus knew 'all men' and what was *within* all men and women (John 2:24–25). Jesus therefore did not entrust himself to people. In other words, he had a robust doctrine of sin. This is why no person in history understood human nature as Jesus did – and why he is never surprised at what people do or when they do it. This is why Jesus does not get disillusioned with you and me! As Gerald Coates says, God never had any illusions of us in the first place! No person understood people as Jesus did and this is why Jesus was the greatest leader in history.

Coping with jealousy

Jesus saw through his enemies and understood them – that they were jealous (Mark 15:10). He also experienced sibling rivalry. Jesus had brothers, and they accused him of carnal ambition – that he wanted to be famous. When Jesus was in Galilee they urged him to go to Jerusalem so that his followers could see him perform miracles. Then came a cutting remark: 'No one who wants to become a public figure acts in secret . . . show yourself to the world' (John 7:4). This was intended as a put-down, and it was hurtful. But 'his own brothers did not believe in him' (v. 5) – at least not then. Jesus did not respond unkindly to them – or say, 'Your problem is that you are jealous' – but only said, 'My time is not yet here; for you any time will do. The world cannot hate you, but it hates me because I testify that its works are evil' (John 7:6–7). Jesus knew their feelings and understood why they made these sharp comments, but he let them save face. He did not walk away or stop talking; he spoke the truth to them without letting on that he knew their real problem. Jealousy in fact lay at the bottom of the Jews' desire to crucify Jesus (Matt. 27:18), but he never accused them of envy or jealousy. (For the reader who would like to delve into this issue more deeply, see my book on jealousy: *The Sin No One Talks About*.)

Brilliant silence

There is a 'time to be silent' (Eccles. 3:7), and Jesus gave a beautiful display of silence before King Herod. When Pilate delivered Jesus to Herod, the latter was rather chuffed to get to see Jesus. He hoped Jesus would perform a miracle for him – like a magician pulling a rabbit out of a hat. Royals are used to people bowing, scraping and fawning over them. In the case of King Herod, many feared him. Jesus merely stood and, possibly, looked Herod right in the eye – Herod was intimidated by him. Then Herod put many questions to Jesus. No reply; silence (Luke 23:8–9).

Jesus did not answer the Roman governor Pontius Pilate at times. When the governor asked, 'Are you the king of the Jews?', Jesus replied: 'You have said so.' But when Jesus was accused by the chief priests and the elders, he gave them no answer. Then Pilate asked him, 'Don't you hear the testimony they are bringing against you?' But Jesus gave no reply, not even to a single charge – 'to the great amazement of the governor' (Matt. 27:11–15). As Isaiah foresaw it hundreds of years before, 'He was oppressed and afflicted, yet he did not open his mouth; he was led like a lamb to the slaughter, and as a sheep before its shearers is silent, so he did not open his mouth' (Isa. 53:7).

Remember too that Jesus' silence was being orchestrated by the Father in heaven; Jesus only spoke when the Father led him to do so. But there is a time to be silent, and there is often more wisdom in silence than in the choicest selection of words. I cannot be sure why Jesus chose to be silent at certain times, but the greatest freedom is having nothing to prove. Jesus was in any case exercising his freedom not to speak.

Can we have Jesus' wisdom?

The final question I want to address is: how can you and I have the wisdom of Jesus? It comes by the fear of the Lord; by heeding the Word of God. That as always is the beginning of wisdom. But that said, there are three principles in the New Testament that show us the way to have Jesus' wisdom.

First, Jesus said if you want to get your theology right, have a right relationship with God: do the will of God. 'If anyone's will is to do God's will, he will know whether the teaching is from God or whether I am speaking on my own authority' (John 7:17, ESV). The key to godly wisdom and sound theology is to be totally resigned to God's will and to do it. I think of countless people in seminaries and universities today who aspire to be theologians and assume erudition is the key. It is not. The key to wisdom and sound, solid theology is to have a personal and intimate relationship with God.

Second, Peter said, '. . . add to your faith goodness; and to goodness, knowledge; and to knowledge, self-control; and to self-control, perseverance; and to perseverance, godliness, and to godliness, mutual affection; and to mutual affection, love. For if you possess these qualities in increasing measure, they will keep you from being ineffective and unproductive in your *knowledge* of our Lord Jesus Christ' (2 Pet. 1:5–8 – my italics). If you want Christ's wisdom and good theology, live a godly life. But there is more; you will receive a 'rich welcome into the eternal kingdom of our Lord and Saviour Jesus Christ' (2 Pet. 1:11). This verse shows that one who receives a rich welcome *has come into their inheritance* along the way. They are those who will receive a wonderful reward at the judgment seat of Christ.

Third, by sharing your faith. 'I pray that your partnership with us in the faith may be effective in deepening your understanding of every good thing we share for the sake of Christ' (Philemon 6). This is one of the most encouraging motivations to be a soul winner of any verse in the New Testament.

Jesus' wisdom not only fulfilled the Law, but also carried out all the wise words to be found in the books of Proverbs and Ecclesiastes. However, if all you do is to aim for the wisdom of Proverbs, you will come short of it. But if you aim for the wisdom of Jesus, focusing non-stop on him and his teachings, you will come the closest that a person can in keeping the sayings of these Old Testament books.

We won't be perfect in this life. We will never outgrow the need of mercy. We will never fully attain to the wisdom of Jesus. But you *can* come closer and closer. Moreover, your light will shine before all people and will glorify your Father in heaven.

Conclusion

> ... since they hated knowledge and did not
> choose to fear the LORD. Since they would not
> accept my advice and spurned my rebuke, they
> will eat the fruit of their ways and be filled with
> the fruit of their schemes. (Prov. 1:29–31)

> The fear of the LORD is the beginning
> of wisdom, and knowledge of the Holy
> One is understanding. (Prov. 9:10)

We have seen that godly wisdom is a secret – an absolute secret that God withholds from everybody – until, that is, he gives it. He alone knows the next step forward for each one of us. He alone knows the end from the beginning (Isa. 46:10). He alone has the exact answer regarding what you should do with your life. He knows what you should say and when to say it. It is the presence of *his* mind that you and I need. He knows how to get things done.

He gives wisdom to those who *choose* the fear of the

Lord. The fear of the Lord is therefore a choice we make in order to have the wisdom I have written about in this book.

It is decision time, and the time is now. Joshua urged the people of ancient Israel, '. . . choose for yourselves this day whom you will serve' (Josh. 24:15). I am going to ask you to pause here. First, if you were to stand before God (and you will) and he were to ask you (he could), 'Why should I let you into heaven?', what would you say? Only one answer will do: that you are trusting in the blood of Jesus which he shed on the cross for your sins. If you have never done so, please pray this prayer:

> Lord Jesus Christ, I need you. I want you. I am sorry for my sins. Wash my sins away by your blood. I welcome your Holy Spirit. As best as I know how I give you my life. Amen.

If you feel that what I have put to you in this book is valid and trustworthy – and consistent with Scripture – commit yourself today to the fear of the Lord. Pray this prayer before the Most High God:

> I commit myself this day to the fear of the Lord. In Jesus' name. Amen.

If you do this – and never rescind – your life will never be the same again.

May the grace and tender mercy of God the Father, God the Son and God the Holy Spirit be with you now and for ever more. Amen.

Do you wish this wasn't the end?
Are you hungry for more great teaching, inspiring
testimonies, ideas to challenge your faith?

Join us at www.hodderfaith.com, follow us on Twitter
or find us on Facebook to make sure you get the latest from
your favourite authors.

Including interviews, videos, articles, competitions
and opportunities to tell us just what you thought about
our latest releases.

www.hodderfaith.com

 HodderFaith

@HodderFaith

 HodderFaithVideo

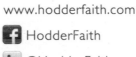

HODDER
WHERE FAITH IS INSPIRED